"Penetrate[s] the mystery of this ancient text on leadership, demonstrating how to turn today's workplace into a source of financial and emotional fulfillment."

—*Shambhala Sun*

"*Real Power* is a guidebook no serious person can afford to miss. It will change the way you work and deepen the way you live."

—Rachel Naomi Remen, M.D., *New York Times* bestselling author of *Kitchen Table Wisdom*

"This book offers the wisest business advice you will ever find—eminently practical and profoundly empowering. The Tao brings true freshness, clarity, and a love of work to employer and employee alike."

—Jack Kornfield, author of *A Path with Heart*

"A remarkable constellation of qualities. A book to have near at hand, day by day, to savor a few pages at a time. It gives a threefold benefit: the wisdom of one of the world's greatest texts, a magnificent contemporary translation, and the thoughts and hard-won experience of a tried-and-true business leader who is also a fine poet."

—David Whyte, author of
*The Heart Aroused: Poetry and the Preservation
of the Soul in Corporate America*

An Alternate Selection of One Spirit Book Club

Real Power

Business Lessons

from the

Tao Te Ching

JAMES A. AUTRY
and STEPHEN MITCHELL

RIVERHEAD BOOKS
New York

RIVERHEAD BOOKS
Published by The Berkley Publishing Group
A member of Penguin Putnam Inc.
375 Hudson Street
New York, New York 10014

First Riverhead hardcover edition: April 1998
First Riverhead trade paperback edition: March 1999
Riverhead trade paperback ISBN: 1-57322-720-X

The Penguin Putnam Inc. World Wide Web site address is
http://www.penguinputnam.com

The Library of Congress has catalogued the Riverhead hardcover edition
as follows:

Autry, James A.
Real power : business lessons from the Tao Te Ching / by
James A. Autry and Stephen Mitchell.
p.   cm.
ISBN 1-57322-089-2
1. Management—Philosophy. 2. Taoism. 3. Success in business.
4. Lao-tzu. Tao Te Ching. I. Mitchell, Stephen, date. II. Title.
HD31.A83   1998   97-32960 CIP
658—dc21

Printed in the United States of America

10   9   8   7   6   5   4   3   2   1

To our dear friends at The Gully

Contents

Preface

I spent a lot of my life looking for answers. As a businessman for thirty-two years, including thirty years in management, I've started new products and renewed old ones, bought successful businesses and sold underperforming ones. I've hired people and promoted people; I've fired people and demoted people. I've managed a staff of ten, and I've managed a group of nine hundred.

For twenty of those years, I maintained the illusion that I could find the answers and be in control. When I finally realized that I couldn't be in control and that, if I was patient, answers would find me, I began the most vibrant, creative, and productive years of my business and personal life.

In my current work with businesses of all sizes, however, I observe that the quest for answers and for control still dominates the thinking of most managers and would-be leaders. Despite all the talk about flattened organizations, dispersed decision-making and empowerment, it's clear that most business people are just more comfortable with the old model.

The command/control system is a tough habit for business to kick. It seems almost comical these days to see on someone's office wall a copy of the company's Christmas tree organization chart. Anyone who has ever spent even a year in business knows that these charts don't reflect how information and power flow in an organization. Yet there they are, like totems, for all to see, as if by seeing them the managers and employees will understand how the organization works.

The organization charts symbolize a larger problem. The charts reflect the ego's short-term desire for power, which it thinks it will get by trying to control things. The top-down management model supports the ego needs of managers, particularly those who don't trust their own abilities to help others become productive.

The great power quest provides a fertile opportunity for the increasing army of management authors and consultants. The result is an outpouring of books about management and leadership that now competes with popular fiction for bookstore shelf space. When one of these books appears, many executives jump at the latest promise of sure-fire prosperity, a new consulting group is born, and business people all over the country find themselves forced to embrace yet another management flavor-of-the-year.

There may be merit in all these systems, but we in the business world have often been disappointed by their failure to live up to their promises. Why do they fail? I believe it is because managers put too much faith in systems and not enough faith in people. Without the commitment and engagement of people, not just at the top but throughout an organization, no system can succeed. The power of any idea is expressed only through people.

I have quoted the Tao Te Ching for years as a senior corporate executive and as a consultant, in speeches and management seminars. Often I have been asked to interpret what a particular chapter meant in a business situation. Other times I have heard the Tao Te Ching criticized as another of those obscure Asian philosophy books being foisted off as New Age management theory.

In the most profound and fundamental sense, the Tao Te Ching is a self-help book. But it often requires adaptation into the business context. When Stephen Mitchell—whose English version of the Tao Te Ching has been called "definitive for our time"—asked if I would be interested in working with him on an interpretation of it for business people, I jumped at the chance.

The Tao Te Ching, perhaps the world's most profound book of leadership wisdom, talks about principles that underlie all truly fulfilling enterprises. It is a way that many powerful business leaders already practice but call by other names, such as "servant leadership" or "values-based leadership" or "leadership from the heart." Each of these phrases describes aspects of the wisdom in this ancient text. It supersedes all systems yet brings fulfillment, both personal and organizational.

· · ·

Though the Tao Te Ching is ancient, the application of its teachings to business leadership is a relatively recent development. At a deep level, the teachings of the Tao Te Ching offer a path that is powerful in a way that conventional business thinking can't be. These teachings point to the most elemental human truths, and they can illuminate any area of human activity. Imagine applying the war metaphors so popular in business circles to your marriage, or taking a manual on how to manage government employees and using it to raise your child. Good luck!

The Tao Te Ching is not asking you to take anything on faith. You don't need to understand all its teachings. Just keep an open mind and test them. The more you are able to live them, the more you will appreciate their profound wisdom and effectiveness.

Business people who have already begun to live these teachings have discovered that they have enormous value not only for their work but for their personal lives as well. This has never been more important. Facing the enormous pressures of business today, many people try to balance their lives and work by allocating certain amounts of time for each. Time is important, but it is far more necessary that you—rather than your time—be balanced. This means being grounded and consistent, manifesting the same values wherever you are, at home or at work, with friends or children, with colleagues, employees, or customers.

Even if you are not facing adversity in your business, all of us in business increasingly face the great unknown. Change is hitting us between the eyes every day. Social change, marketplace change, legislative change, financial change, and the most intrusive of them all, technological change. The overarching truth of all this change is that we don't know what is going to happen, we're not sure we'll know what to do, and we can't even be confident that our businesses or our jobs will be relevant five years from now.

The Tao Te Ching teaches that true understanding is realizing that you have nowhere to stand. I can't think of a more compelling time to seek the wisdom of the Tao Te Ching and to become comfortable with the reality that the acceptance of non-control is the only way to manage things. Read about, think about, and embrace the concept of not-knowing. Then you'll be able to face, as you never have before, this insane pace of change.

There is no special technique and no special knowledge required for getting what you need from this book. Start anywhere. Dip in. Read the same chapter several times to see how many different lessons you can learn. Keep it in your desk. Carry it in your briefcase.

In commenting on the text, I have tried to adapt Lao-tzu's examples of governance and military strategy to business leadership situations. You'll find commentary on downsizing, compensation, appraisals, training, acquisitions, competition, and many other contemporary business topics. I hope this interpretation will serve as a bridge for business people while remaining true to the meaning of the original text. My objective is simple: to give business people and leaders a powerful tool for tapping into the most important resource they have—their own wisdom.

—JAMES A. AUTRY

Foreword

The Tao Te Ching—pronounced "*Dow* (no pun intended) *Deh Jing*"—teaches a wisdom that was ancient even for Lao-tzu, its perhaps legendary author, who did or didn't write it around the year 500 B.C.E. Though it was almost unknown in the West until the twentieth century, it is by now the most widely translated book in the world, aside from the Bible. It has been called the wisest book ever written. It is also the most practical book ever written. In eighty-one brief chapters, the Tao Te Ching looks at the basic predicament of being human and gives advice that imparts balance and perspective, a serene and generous spirit. It teaches how to work for the good with the effortless skill that comes from being in accord with reality, and it applies equally well to the governing of a nation or the raising of a child. It is the classic manual on the art of living, written in a style of gemlike lucidity, radiant with humor and grace and largeheartedness and deep wisdom: one of the wonders of the world.

Like all realms of human activity, business and management can be powerfully illuminated by the teaching of the Tao Te Ching. But the text is so dense, so packed with essence, that its relevance may at first be hard to see. That is why Jim Autry and I decided to select these passages and adapt them for business people (the numbers at the bottom of the selections are the chapter numbers in the original version). The commentary—Jim's mostly, with suggestions by me—is an unpacking and a filling-out of certain aspects of the text. Of course, the Tao Te Ching is deeper and wider than any explanation of it could be. After reading each chapter of commentary, you may also want to spend some time with the text, by itself, even—or especially—when it seems impenetrable. What is impenetrable today may be crystal-clear tomorrow. It grows clear as you put it into practice.

Many people, in their first encounters with the Tao Te Ching, get stuck on the word *Tao*. Literally it means "the Way," and it indicates the way things are, the source or essence or basic principle of the universe. You may find this difficult to grasp. Actually, it's impossible to grasp. That's the point! Anything words can say about it isn't it. It's unthinkable, unimaginable, un-pin-downable.

There was something formless and perfect
before the universe was born.
It is serene. Empty.
Solitary. Unchanging.
Infinite. Eternally present.
It flows through all things,

inside and outside, and returns
to the origin of all things.
It is the mother of the universe.
For lack of a better name,
I call it the Tao.

> (from Chapter 25 of the original,
> not included in our selection)

The Tao isn't an idea. Nor is it some kind of airy-fairy mystical imagining. Even though you can't perceive it, it is always present, always with you. "The Tao is the law of nature," another ancient classic says, "which your true self can't depart from even for one instant. If you could depart from it, it wouldn't be the Tao." It is the realest of the real. You can't see it, but you can see its effects, the way physicists can trace the path of a sub-atomic particle through a cloud chamber. With a little practice, you'll find it easy to sense when you're in harmony with the Tao and when you're going against its current.

We all know, from our experience of sports or dance, what it's like to be "in the Tao" or "in the zone": caught up in the current of energy where the right action happens by itself, effortlessly. Somehow the innate intelligence of the body takes over for a while, and the ball throws the ball, the racquet swings the racquet, we can't tell the dancer from the dance. This is a paradigm for what the Tao Te Ching calls "not-doing" or "non-action": the purest and most effective form of action. It is always a magical experience. If you think about it, you lose it. If you try to make it happen, it won't. It comes and goes at its own sweet pleasure. When it comes, we are thrilled and grateful. When it's gone, we try to do our ordinary best. The central lesson here is to let go of control, to let go of even the desire to control. When the ego steps out of the way, the Tao steps in, intelligent beyond our dreams.

The more you embody these teachings, the more the scattered parts of your life fall into place and become a seamless whole; work seems effortless; your heart opens by itself to all the people in your life; you have time for everything worthwhile; your mind becomes empty, transparent, serene; you embrace sorrow as much as joy, failure as much as success; you unthinkingly act with integrity and compassion; and you find that you have come to trust life completely.

Lao-tzu's central figure, which he calls the Master, is a man or a woman whose life is in perfect harmony with the way things are. She or he is the opposite of an idealist or a mystic; is in fact infinitely down-to-earth, capable, flexible, sexy, humorous, loving, and radiantly alive. The Master, the mature person, the wise leader, is a reality that can be embodied by each one of us. We are all potentially the Master, since the Master is the essential us, seeing all things with our original face. Nothing in the world is as beautiful as this face. If you look in the mirror with enough patience, that's the one you will see.

—STEPHEN MITCHELL

Real Power

Prologue

—1—

The tao that can be told
is not the eternal Tao.
The name that can be named
is not the eternal Name.

The unnamable is the eternally real. . . .

(from Chapter 1)

Some business leaders just have it. You know it when you see it but you can't really identify it or classify it. You might call it judgment or instinct or intuition; you may say it's the "touch" or the "knack." You can't put your finger on it, and you don't know what to call it. The fact is, it doesn't have a name. And that's okay, as long as you are able to see for yourself what happens when leaders know how to be: a particular CEO or executive VP or department head just has a way of making things turn out okay for everybody in the group while achieving excellent business results. Not that every idea or plan or product is a rousing success, but the leader and the employees accept the outcome, learn from it, and move on to the next project with passion and enthusiasm.

If you look beyond the workplace, you find that the leaders and employees are fulfilled not only by their work but in their personal lives as well. They are passionately involved in their communities, and they experience deep joy and connection with their loved ones.

When you see all these results, you are seeing the good work of wise leaders. Despite attempts to explain the success of these leaders, the characteristics that bring it about are not explainable. Business school scholars do case studies from time to time, trying to define what they think they observe in order to replicate it as a system. Then to the dismay of the scholars, it—whatever "it" is—doesn't work in another setting or with another manager.

What is most valuable doesn't have a name. The wise leader is comfortable with the mystery of that and doesn't waste energy trying to figure it out. She doesn't need to label everything and doesn't let herself be limited by the desire for any particular result. She knows that her job is to bring people together in the workplace and, through training as well as through personal encouragement, to assure that they understand how their individual jobs connect with the greater purpose of the business. Once that's done, she trusts that committed people working together in a community of effort will produce more than she could ever have prescribed through a formal strategic planning process. This is the basis for real power.

Part I

The Wise Leader

2

If you want to become whole,
let yourself be partial.
If you want to become straight,
let yourself be crooked.
If you want to become full,
let yourself be empty. . . .

(from Chapter 22)

Think of yourself as a work in progress. Because we all are. And it is a major step toward wholeness to accept our incompleteness. When we recognize that very fact, we become more complete.

Whatever it is you have in life—talent, resources, position—that is enough. If you truly accept that you have enough of everything, those gifts will multiply throughout your organization and will be used in the most supportive and caring way. You may receive more of everything, to be sure; you may enjoy what you receive. That's just fine. Go ahead and celebrate the abundance, all the perceived symbols of success, everything from a luxury car to a condo in some vacation spot. But don't get hung up on whether you have this stuff or not, and never lament what you don't have. That kind of thinking will keep you from realizing that with all your incompleteness you are always whole.

There was a very successful businessman, not well educated but a shrewd and savvy executive who had made a series of profitable acquisitions and had built a substantial string of automobile service stations. But he was known among colleagues and friends as perpetually dissatisfied with his business record. He'd drive by a competitor's station and say, "I could have had that operation for a fraction of its cost today," or "I had a chance at that one, but I was too dumb to take it." Then one day late in his life, he stopped in the midst of one of these speeches and said to a friend, "You know, you can't make a penny on those damn coulda-had stations." And he never mentioned them again.

You can't gain anything from worrying about what you didn't get or don't have.

Where does real power begin? On the inside, with self-awareness and self-acceptance. It is a transition from the external to the internal. Accepting things as they are, accepting yourself as you are—this is the pathway to leadership and fulfillment.

3

Men are born soft and supple;
dead, they are stiff and hard.
Plants are born tender and pliant;
dead, they are brittle and dry.

Thus whoever is stiff and inflexible
is a disciple of death.
Whoever is soft and yielding
is a disciple of life. . . .

(from Chapter 76)

We generally admire people in business who are organized and buttoned up. Stiffness—"sticking to your guns" and so on—is often interpreted as masculine "strength." But it's often true that these same people are inflexible in their attitudes. It's important to ask whether they are organized and buttoned up because they're efficient or because they're afraid of not being in control.

Softness, on the other hand, represents feminine "weakness." But we'd do well to drop the guns and forget these stereotypes. Not only are they silly but they are inaccurate and misleading. Softness can also mean suppleness, flexibility, openness of body and mind. Watch a t'ai chi or aikido master if you want to know how powerful softness in action can be.

Managers often find their suppleness challenged when confronting situations that violate their expectations of how things should be. For example, some managers consider it a personal betrayal if someone, particularly a key person, resigns. "After all I've done," the manager thinks, "she takes another job and disrupts all my plans for her and the department."

Then there are managers who are stunned when business conditions shift, or the marketplace takes a turn that the strategic plan didn't cover in the "contingencies" section. They can't cope with a reality beyond their ability to predict, so they either overreact or become paralyzed.

The wise leader makes use of difficulties like a resignation, realizing that every time an employee comes or goes, there is an opportunity, perhaps to change the organizational structure, to give another employee a promotion, or yes, even to eliminate a job and cut costs. When an employee resigns, the leader wishes that person well and never shuts the door to re-employment.

A CEO of a very successful large retail company actively encourages his salespeople to use their own judgment in dealing with customers, keeping in mind that retaining the customer is more important than store policies or regulations. Most retailers establish rigid procedures for every transaction, thus transforming their salespeople into dull extensions of an inflexible system. When asked if his softness toward customers costs more in extra exchanges or encourages the salespeople to "give away the store," he responded that abusive behavior which arises from adhering to a system for its own sake drives away so many customers that he comes out ahead.

The wise leader knows that it is absurd to believe he can plan for every contingency, and that there are great opportunities if he remains flexible and makes use of whatever happens. In fact, the best solutions often come in response to the unplanned-for situation, because those solutions arise from the leader's deeper intelligence.

Just as body and mind stay young and vital by increasing their flexibility, an organization that values suppleness stays vital and creative. It is an act of strength to let go of old definitions of power and to remain flexible, soft, and ready to yield.

4

Can you coax your mind from its wandering
and keep to the original oneness?
Can you let your body become
supple as a newborn child's?
Can you cleanse your inner vision
until you see nothing but the light? . . .

(from Chapter 10)

I t's difficult to remain focused on the open and spacious atmosphere necessary to create the best working environments. We all know how easily distracted the mind can be—especially when in the midst of one project, a crisis or call to arms in which we might be the hero fractures our concentration.

Some people, of course, need a crisis, and if a crisis isn't happening, they'll create one. They'll eagerly search the in box for a problem, or they'll imbue a project with false urgency because they need a crisis as something to react to; they need it to feel as if they're really doing something; and they need it as an excuse for substandard work. "I could have done a better job, but we were right up against the wall. We're lucky to have gotten this project done at all."

These folks like to claim that a situation is impossible, so that the boss will appreciate their can-do attitude for attempting the impossible. There was a very successful senior manager who, when told a project was impossible, always asked, "Is it impossible or merely inconvenient?" Most of the time, it was merely inconvenient.

People who are driven by crisis are letting circumstances define their lives instead of allowing all things to arise in the space in which work is performed. They may succeed for a while and rise to a certain level of distinction as crisis managers, but at what price? They forget how to function in the "normal" mode. They never understand what it means to do excellent work and to find fulfillment in it. They lose the capacity to be reflective—to see the space out of which all great wisdom and work is born.

We often have to shift gears many times in a day or a week, and if we can't do it fluidly, we create more difficulty for ourselves by clinging to the first project while being pulled toward the next, all the time doing battle with our own sense of priority. As our minds come to resemble the new work environment, we become supple enough to allow for all circumstances, without being divided internally.

— 5 —

Those who know don't talk.
Those who talk don't know. . . .

Be like the Tao.
It can't be approached or withdrawn from,
benefited or harmed,
honored or brought into disgrace.
It gives itself up continually.
That is why it endures.

(from Chapter 56)

The spoken exchange of information is such an important part of business that it inspires us to talk too much—as if the more said about a subject the better. Yet every salesperson has had the experience of losing a sale because he didn't know when to shut up and let the customer say "yes."

Managers talk too much because they think that they're supposed to have all the answers, but talking too much frequently deprives them of information. When the leader is talking, most people will keep quiet. A manager's silence, on the other hand, liberates everyone else to speak. Ask questions, then be quiet, even if the answers aren't immediately blurted out. Resisting the compulsion to fill these silences can elicit responses you would never have gotten otherwise.

Encourage your group to sit in silence for a few minutes. You'll be surprised by what reveals itself when the conversation begins again. It is often the heartfelt and truly urgent comment that emerges to break a silence. You may find out that a key person on a project didn't know what was expected; or that there were not enough resources, or they had the wrong resources; perhaps you underestimated, or overestimated, the work load; perhaps someone has a better way of accomplishing the task at hand but didn't speak up because you always gave them the answers. If you're talking instead of listening, you'll never know what situations truly require your attention.

One very successful company schedules a special meeting every month in every department. It's called the "circles of silence" meeting and is designed to give everyone a chance to talk about subjects *other than* logistics, planning, operations, and budget. As the CEO explains, "We begin with twenty minutes of complete silence which, studies have shown, changes the brain chemistry. Whether that's true or not, I know it creates a different emotional atmosphere. We talk about how we're feeling about our work, our lives, anything. A lot of stuff comes out, some conflict even, but we're able to talk it through." What are the benefits? "For one thing, we get to know one another better; you could even say that we get to care about one another. This creates a more positive intent in the working relationship, and it seems to eliminate a lot of griping and backbiting, because we have a forum in which all that gets an open, honest airing."

Contrast this attitude with that of another top corporate executive who became known for making poor hiring decisions. He would ask a candidate a question, and when the person hesitated, the executive would begin to talk. If the candidate smiled, nodded, and seemed to be in agreement with what the executive was saying, this man assumed a level of intelligence and ability in the candidate for which he had no evidence.

One of the great steps toward real power is learning when to speak and when to remain quiet. And when you do speak, use straightforward, simple language. The objective should be clear communication. Use the same voice and manner with everyone, whether they are managers, employees, or colleagues. Be relaxed, centered, grounded, calm.

If you can achieve this thoughtful way of communicating, your perspective and sense of balance will never be affected by the vagaries of your professional or personal world, by changes in people or organizations, by good news or bad.

6

As it acts in the world, the Tao
is like the bending of a bow.
The top is bent downward;
the bottom is bent up.
It adjusts excess and deficiency
so that there is perfect balance. . . .

(from Chapter 77)

The majority of heart attacks occur around nine on Monday mornings. One study showed that the most common factor in these heart attacks was that the victims were people whose work had become "joyless striving." In other words, they couldn't find meaning in their work, and their lives had become so out of balance that, one Monday morning, their bodies said, "You're not going to work today. Zap."

There is a CEO who's fond of saying, "My job is to create stress." Then, of course, he starts complaining about the high cost of health care in his company. He must be the last person to see the connection between stress and health problems.

The universe strives for balance. It doesn't allow things to pile up for very long. Not even for business people. How many times do hard-driving managers get struck by stress-related illnesses? How many times have you heard, "A heart attack is God's way of telling you to slow down"?

When your life is out of balance, nothing works. There's too much pressure on the job and too much pressure at home and not enough time to respond to either. In the quest for a balanced life, most business people are frustrated to the point that their conversations are often preoccupied with just how miserably they fail at it. They strive for "quality" time with family and friends, for networking time with business associates, for productive work time, and for time to just think. They seem to believe that, if there were just more hours added to every day, their lives would miraculously become balanced.

One senior executive made it a practice to intervene when he noticed someone at the office nights and weekends on a regular basis. The executive would examine the job description and the performance standards of that person to determine what required so much time. His assumption was always that if there's a job that requires this much time to accomplish, there must be something wrong with the way the job is set up. He explained, "If you let employees work this long and hard, you'll eventually lose your training investment in them, because they'll either burn out or leave, or both."

Turnover from burnout is wasted money, and it's always management's fault. Pushing employees, or yourself, so hard to be productive that you create an unhealthy environment is anything *but* productive.

Balancing your life is not about time; it's about values. You may learn helpful ways to make better use of your time, but your life won't become balanced until you also learn to determine what you truly value.

The ancient Masters were profound and subtle.
Their wisdom was unfathomable.
There is no way to describe it;
all we can describe is their appearance.

They were careful
as someone crossing an iced-over stream.
Alert as a warrior in enemy territory. . . .

Do you have the patience to wait
till your mud settles and the water is clear?
Can you remain unmoving
till the right action arises by itself?

The Master doesn't seek fulfillment.
Not seeking, not expecting,
she is present, and can welcome all things.

(from Chapter 15)

Of all the words written about how a leader acts and is, these are the simplest yet most profound. They may be difficult to fully achieve, but we can all begin to put them into practice.

Many managers might consider themselves careful and alert in the sense that they are always watching their employees to make sure they don't do something wrong, or that they are always protecting themselves from blame. The images of thin ice and enemy territory aren't about a threat to the manager's status or authority. Rather, they are about an alertness and sensitivity that enhances the state of being completely attentive to everything and everyone around you—in particular, attentive to the appropriate time for action.

It's easy enough to say that the wise leader is careful, alert, courteous, flexible, receptive, thoughtful, and open-minded. It's almost like reciting the Boy Scout or Girl Scout code of behavior. But this text really boils down to patience. Managers, conditioned to be decisive, generally act too quickly, whereas not acting at all may be the right action. Some do the wrong thing; others do the right thing but invalidate it by doing it at the wrong time.

"So I'm sitting there," you say, "waiting for the right action and the right time to reveal themselves, and the boss comes in and says, 'You're not doing anything.' Am I supposed to say, 'I'm waiting for the right time, boss'? Yeah, right."

It can be scary to trust that right actions reveal themselves if you are patient and ready to recognize them. The only way to know the right action is to clear your mind of the mud of anger, of fear, of assumptions, and of ambition—the mud of ego, the mud of control. If you can't do that, you'll always take the quick and obvious action, letting the chips fall where they may and hoping for a good batting average—like most other managers in the world.

. . . Think of the small as large
and the few as many.
Confront the difficult
while it is still easy;
accomplish the great task
by a series of small acts. . . .

(from Chapter 63)

F orget the categories of big and small. To engage your job well, indeed to engage life well, you should think of nothing as small and nothing as big. What is small, anyway? Changing a diaper, sweeping up, saying "hello" to an employee? What's big? A strategic planning meeting, a major sales presentation, a conference with the financial analysts?

Each one of these things, from the diaper-changing to the financial conference, could be a cosmic event. We have no way to see the ultimate consequences of even the smallest action, so each one deserves the same meticulous attention. Every action is an integral part of your life or job, and giving it your full attention can make a huge difference in how things work out. Any good parent can see a child's affinities in its small actions or unimportant comments. If those actions are overlooked, a prime opportunity to nurture the child's talents will be lost.

It's important that you think of everything you do in

this way. Most of us remember our mothers doing all the little daily acts of comfort and support—such as bringing a cool cloth when we were sick in the middle of the night—but when business people are asked how many remember their fathers doing those things, very few respond. Think of the chances for connection those fathers missed by not seeing how the small and sometimes not-so-pleasant acts are part of their growth as people and as parents. The same opportunities for growth and connection are there on the job every day.

Preoccupation with the big picture can seduce you into believing that all the details are not worth your attention. Meanwhile, a lot of vital "little" things can fall through the cracks and cause your grand opportunity to come crashing down.

For example, back in the eighties, a well-known publishing company acquired a smaller publisher for a very handsome price. The acquisition was part of a top executive's vision to dominate a certain area of publishing. In the push to make the acquisition and to secure this grand position in the marketplace, the executive pressured his people to act without their usual diligence. "We can sweep up the details later," he told them. However, his people in their rush overlooked one detail that couldn't be swept up. Thousands of customers were ordering the product. The orders were in hand. That was good. The billings were going out on time. That was good. But only twenty percent of the customers were paying their bills. Somehow someone forgot to check the collection rate, which was not exactly concealed but was well buried in a lot of other financial details. That was bad—so bad in fact that the entire strategy fell flat, and the resulting losses precluded other investments for several years.

And how about this question: "Who is little and who is big?" Is the CEO big and the janitor little? People in a hierarchy tend to think this way, but it's a serious mistake, because it inevitably leads those people to assign certain characteristics to the "big" and others to the "small." For instance, the higher-ups must be smarter, right? They must be the ones with the compelling marketing statements or the new product ideas or the innovative production process, right? Wrong. No person in your company has more human worth than another. Regardless of the importance of the job, regardless of income or status, no one is bigger or smaller than anyone else. We have too often confused human worth with the market value of a job, and we have let ego needs distort organizational hierarchy into a social class system within companies.

The higher-ups aren't necessarily the most intelligent people in an organization, but they are probably very good at orchestrating the talents of others. They understand that their role is to bring those talents together with other resources for the good of the enterprise. In fact, the companies that will not only survive but prevail into the next century are those that look to the grass-roots workers for innovation and that recognize and reward those workers regardless of hierarchy.

Even though everyone can be rewarded, not everyone can be paid the same. Be open about the fact that some jobs have more perceived value to the enterprise and are given greater compensation. People can understand that a mail-room job isn't of the same importance to a company's success as is a senior sales position, but they can't understand or accept it when you think of the mail sorter as a "little" person. When this happens, the "little" people become resentful. They lose their commitment to the company because they don't feel valued, though their pay and benefits may be competitive. Unions form not primarily to increase pay and benefits; they arise in situations where employees feel denigrated.

The wise leader understands that when you don't judge what's big or small, every action becomes important. The appropriate question is not "What's big and what's small?" It's "What's next?"

9

For governing a country well
there is nothing better than moderation.

The mark of a moderate man
is freedom from his own ideas. . . .

Nothing is impossible for him.
Because he has let go,
he can care for the people's welfare . . .

(from Chapter 59)

Most people think of themselves as moderate, because they define the moderate person as one who is not extreme, who seeks the middle ground. But moderation is *not* the middle ground. The wise manager, in fact, recognizes that he doesn't have the luxury of the middle ground. He must constantly evaluate ideas and proposals, and he must allocate time and money in support of the ones most likely to benefit the whole enterprise. If he always seeks the middle ground and chooses the most popular ideas or projects, his work may easily become mediocre. So moderation often means letting go of pressures to make the popular choice, and making the best choice.

When it comes to dealing with your employees, moderation means being evenhanded and fair. Choosing one person's ideas over another's may seem to create the impression of a star system, which looks like unfair and immoderate management. It's important to make sure that your people understand the fairness of your longer view. A magazine editor, for instance, can't choose editorial material so that each department gets equal coverage in every issue, despite pressures from individual staff members to do just that. The result would be a magazine that is utterly predictable—and boring. The moderate editor should take the longer view, assuring balance during perhaps six months or a year.

You can avoid the star system by involving everyone to some extent in all projects, by developing an attitude of community within your department, an atmosphere in which everyone feels part of the overall process and in which your people use the words *we* and *our* rather than *I* and *my*. Let people know that when you make one choice now, you are not necessarily rejecting the other for all time.

This kind of moderation results from a difficult and continuing internal process. It requires letting go of all your preconceptions and being ready to make the best of every situation.

—10—

*. . . When people see some things as good,
other things become bad. . . .*

*The Master has but doesn't possess,
acts but doesn't expect. . . .*

(from Chapter 2)

W hen in the interest of classification and control, you put a label on anything, you do two things: You restrict the potential of what you have labeled and, at the same time, you require that its opposite exist. Thus a person can't be good unless someone else is bad. The same with right or wrong, winner or loser.

In effect, what you do is put on the filters of your preconceptions. For instance, as a manager, you see performance through the filter of the "right way to do things." You judge a junior manager's potential through the filter of "what an up-and-coming person should look and act like." You evaluate an employee's performance through the filter of "how I would have done that job."

All these filters have one ostensible purpose: to distinguish whether things are done right or wrong. Unfortunately for us, our employees, and our businesses, these particular characterizations are not only worthless but also frequently destructive. They hold our people hostage to an inflexible standard that may be out of date or irrelevant or just plain useless in this place and time.

Traditional business concepts of organizational structure and management technique often condition managers to classify and measure everything and everyone they are responsible for. Organizational charts assign names to little boxes in hierarchical order. Job descriptions delineate exactly what everyone is supposed to do. Performance standards focus activities on a list of goals to be accomplished within a certain time. Performance appraisals rate performance according to a numerical scale, which then determines the percentage of salary increase. On paper, it's all very tidy.

Not that there is no value in all these charts and systems; on the contrary, they offer a worthwhile way of understanding the fundamental structure. But the structure should serve, as chords do in jazz, as a basis for innovation and improvisation. The CEO of a very successful media company has a unique approach. He begins as any other manager would, by hiring a person to accomplish a specific set of tasks, then he encourages the new employee to look beyond those tasks to find other things that need doing and that she is enthusiastic about doing. Only later do the CEO and the employee choose a job title.

Another CEO decided to add a training and development position for his rapidly growing staff, but he was convinced that if he limited the job to training and development, it could quickly become bureaucratic and stuck in old models of how to train people. After finding the person who he thought grasped his concept of the job, he worked with her to come up with a title. None of the regular titles seemed open-ended enough, so they settled on "VP of Transformation and Discovery." Despite a few snickers from both inside and outside the company, the job has worked out very well.

We get stuck on titles, but it is the rare job title that accurately describes all the functions an employee performs. Jobs change, yet because the titles tend to tell people how they should define what they do, it's not unusual to find employees hanging on to old definitions of their jobs when the business climate demands new definitions. Thus we end up disciplining or firing people for not doing what they didn't know they should have done.

Huge problems arise when managers use the structure to oppress creativity in the name of organizational tidiness. They question any activity that doesn't fit their preconceptions. They ask, "Why are you doing that? It's not in your job description." The result is that people define their jobs narrowly. The last thing you want to have is an atmosphere in which people avoid doing something innovative or something that simply needs to be done because "it's not my job."

It's an illusion to think that if we can put all things in just the right category, we can control them. If you believe this, you're kidding yourself. Regardless of what the organization chart shows, regardless of the authority you as a manager have to make assignments or to allocate resources, you are not in control of people. People control their own behavior or it doesn't get controlled. You are not in control of how customers choose to spend their money. You are not in control of stock prices. Or interest rates. Or the supply of raw materials. Or the availability of talented employees. A preoccupation with control is counterproductive to everything business leaders need to accomplish.

In order to be a wise leader, you should abandon preconceptions. You should evaluate people on the basis of the results of their work and not on how you think they should have done it, how you would have done it, or whether it conforms to the conventional way of doing it, or even conforms to their job description.

And you should never evaluate your employees according to the bell curve. The bell curve is just another way of labeling people and their work. It assumes that some of your employees will always be stars, others will be benchwarmers, but most will be mediocre.

Naturally you will be aware of differences in the work of different employees, but you should use this knowledge to assure that all employees are assigned to do what they do best, in the best interest of all.

11

. . . He who has power over others
can't empower himself.
He who clings to his work
will create nothing that endures.

If you want to accord with the Tao,
just do your job, then let go.

(from Chapter 24)

Managers who believe that power comes from authority risk losing their power altogether. It's just as likely that employees will take away a manager's power as it is that a manager will disempower employees. If you are too directive, if you constantly tell your employees what to do and how to do it, if you look over their shoulders—if, in other words, you act as a supervisor rather than as a manager—you're asking for trouble.

One senior manager, new to the job, learned the hard way. He came in on the first day telling his department heads what he thought should be done. He didn't ask. They, of course, knew that his ideas had been tried and wouldn't work, but because they'd been told and not asked, they simply did as he said. In about a month, they returned and said, "Sorry, we tried but it didn't work." The boss found himself thoroughly disempowered and had to start all over again with a different approach.

But, you may ask, if power doesn't come from authority, what good is authority?

Authority is only the vehicle. It is the means to achieving power but not the power itself. The people with the most authority in a company are not always the people with the most power. A profit-center manager who is making great profits and returns will generally have more influence with top management—and maybe even more income—than a senior vice president on the corporate staff. From the company's point of view, your objective is to achieve results, and the company vests you with authority in order for you to achieve those results. So power, which comes to you from the results you achieve, is simply part of the return on the company's investment in your authority.

The wise leader never forgets this: that authority may be pleasing to the ego, but real power comes from results, and results come from the people.

The fact is that conventional business understanding of empowerment is based on two false assumptions: (1) that empowerment is about moving decision making and freedom of action to "lower levels" in the company; and (2) that you as a manager have power and are going to give some of it to your employees, thus empowering them.

But real empowerment is not about taking power from the top and spreading it through the company. On the contrary, it is about you as a manager recognizing that your employees already have power. It is the power of their skills, their commitment to the job, and their passion for the work. This is not your power to give. Real power is power that you can recognize and honor by creating an environment in which that power can be expressed for the good of all. It is power *with* your people, not power *over* your people. In the same way, your own power comes not from your authority but from your abilities, experience, and commitment. The real job of empowerment is bringing the power of your employees together with your own power in order to produce the best results for everyone.

12

. . . Can you step back from your own mind
and thus understand all things?

Giving birth and nourishing,
having without possessing,
acting with no expectations,
leading and not trying to control:
this is the supreme virtue.

(from Chapter 10)

The most important understanding we can have about work is not that we are there to cultivate ideas, but that we are there to cultivate the space that holds ideas. Space, emptiness. This is the ground out of which all valuable ideas are born. The more open the space, the more possibilities can arise.

There's just one thing that collapses that space: expectation. When people are talking with the boss, they are always aware of hierarchy, so they measure their words and actions, assuming that they are constantly being judged. This is, in fact, most often the case, and the added self-consciousness can stifle someone's best ideas. But if people feel that they can be themselves, that they aren't being judged against the boss's preconceptions, then they become liberated to do their best work. When you can act in this way to support people and ideas, you will be creating an atmosphere that gives birth to high morale and productivity.

Stepping back from your own mind means also stepping from content into space, stepping back from what you think you know and allowing other opinions, other ideas, other people to be fully present in your awareness. This lets you see them in the light of how they truly are, without the filter of how you think they should be or how you'd like them to be.

Most of us don't realize how much our expectations determine someone else's behavior, and many of us don't realize how negative our expectations can be. Many businesses are set up to prevent wrongdoing instead of to encourage rightdoing, but if you can see the best in people and let them know that you see the best in them, they will manifest their best selves.

13

. . . The Master does nothing,
yet he leaves nothing undone.
The ordinary man is always doing things,
yet many more are left to be done.

The kind man does something,
yet something remains undone.
The just man does something,
and leaves many things to be done.
The moral man does something,
and when no one responds
he rolls up his sleeves and uses force. . . .

(from Chapter 38)

In the attempt to become leaders, managers often make faulty assumptions or choose faulty role models of how a leader should look and behave. In effect, they choose a descriptor they want applied to themselves, then they cultivate a false persona that meets that descriptor. They miss the point that being oneself is the strongest persona to have, so rather than becoming extraordinary, they join the populous ranks of the ordinary managers who are unlikely to become leaders.

Businesses are full of the "ordinary man," as the Tao Te Ching puts it, managers who have assumed that the successful business person tries to be everywhere at the same time and never wastes a minute. While driving, they talk on the cell phone; when in the hotel room, they go on-line with e-mail; on vacation, they're always in touch with the office. When times get tough, they get busier. When things go wrong, they get busier. When things are great, they get busier. They are flattered when people describe them as very busy, and when someone says "I hate to bother you because you're so busy," they take it as the ultimate compliment.

There are other versions of the ordinary man:

There's the "kind man," the manager who tries so hard to be a good guy that he seems to wander without a compass, leaving his people to conclude that there are no real standards of performance. He lets them set their own goals without his participation. But by not having goals for them, he fails to understand that a certain amount of structure creates freedom, that people are liberated by guidelines. The "kind man" deludes himself into thinking he is liberating people by not providing a framework, but he is insulting them by his indefiniteness. Of course he is no less power-hungry than the busy man; it's just that he believes that to be liked is to be a leader.

Opposite the "kind man" is the "just man," the manager who is so concerned that everyone be treated fairly that no one is treated particularly well. He turns the framework into a straitjacket by applying exactly the same guidelines to everyone. He makes exceptions for no one and takes pride in treating everyone the same, but this policy is just something to hide behind. It allows him to avoid the hard work of managing people one at a time, rather than in groups, and of responding to their strengths and weaknesses individually. As William Blake said, "One law for the lion and the ox is oppression."

And everyone knows the "moral man." He believes in a rigid set of rules that make every action either right or wrong. Since these rules are objectively true, it is his duty to roll up his sleeves and impose them on others, for their own good, whether or not they assent to his beliefs. The "moral man" often steps over the line by legislating the personal behavior of his people according to his own standards. People may be passed over for advancement because they go to a different church or are having an affair. Rather than simply living his values, the moral man tries to make his definition of morality apply to everyone else.

What happens to a company when these "ordinary men" become dominant in the management culture? If the "kind man" becomes dominant, people leave because they are without direction and purpose. If the "just man" or the "moral man" takes over, the sense that employees will do the right thing if given the opportunity is replaced by the belief that employees must be told what to do and how to behave. This leads to elaborate policies, procedures, and rules—and an atmosphere of prohibition. Then employees, not trusted to use their own judgment, start to believe that if something isn't prohibited, it must be okay. Result: more prohibitions. Further result: a chaotic work culture in which people abandon their judgment of what to do and what not to do, and instead constantly push the definition of what's allowed.

The person who boasts about being a leader isn't one. The true leader doesn't boast about it. He has no ego investment in being a leader; he just is. He knows that his power comes not from authority but from his people, so he uses his position to assure that they have the resources and support they need to do their work. Thus, people give him power, because they know he will use it to benefit everyone and not just himself. This is true power.

In the same way, the wise leader has no ego investment in doing things. This doesn't mean that he loafs on the job. On the contrary, he sees clearly what needs to be done, then applies his intelligence and talent so effectively that it seems things just get done through him. He doesn't make a big deal out of what he's doing at any time. These attitudes are what make him a truly extraordinary business person.

14

The great Way is easy,
yet people prefer the side paths.
Be aware when things are out of balance.
Stay centered within the Tao. . . .

(from Chapter 53)

The wise leader realizes that a company exists in a complex educational, social, economic, and governmental ecosystem, thus it is responsible not only to stockholders but also to employees, customers, vendors, and the community at large. As old-fashioned and self-evident as this may seem, few of today's senior business leaders now practice this kind of balance. Too many of them prefer the side paths of short-term profits and short-term increases in what has been narrowly defined as "stockholder value." This has created a crisis of trust, because two of the most popular shortcuts to profit are also the most disruptive. One is downsizing, and the other is outsourcing.

Downsizing has now caused millions of workers to distrust their companies and to live in constant anxiety about their jobs, because they don't know who will be downsized next. In addition, the rush to cut staff also often cuts research and development and the ability to innovate.

The staff who remain are so overloaded they don't even have time to think. Their creative juices drain away, and they burn out. Any concern for workers' well-being gets lost in the push for more productivity.

Concomitant with downsizing is outsourcing, the hiring of outside firms to furnish services or products once produced inside the company. There may be short-term advantages to your budget, but you can also be sure that your company will have to share any innovations or efficiencies with the supplier's other customers, meaning that there can now be no competitive advantage gained by a new product or process because it wasn't developed within your company, just for your company. The more a company's products or services resemble every other company's products or services, the more everything becomes a commodity. This is already happening, and it will inevitably undermine brands and make everyone compete on price alone. Chaos indeed.

Despite these risks and problems, stock analysts—who are on one of the notorious side paths of business— conclude that, as a result of the layoffs and the expected increase in productivity, the company will prosper. Their analysis then becomes the basis for pushing up the stock price (the reductionist definition of "stockholder value").

Of course, this analysis is mere speculation, but more often than not, it causes a rise in stock price that then results in extravagant stock-option income for those very company officers who decided to cut costs by cutting the workforce.

There's no denying that when a company has become

unprofitable and its survival depends on cost cutting, lay-offs may become necessary. People can understand that. But when a company is making good profits and good returns and then lays off workers as if they're replaceable commodities, while rewarding its officers with big stock options, its reward system has gotten out of whack. This has a pervasive demoralizing impact on every worker at every level. The people feel robbed, and in effect they have been robbed—of their good will, of their sense of connection with the company, of the years they've put into the job. This leads to a loss and not a gain in productivity, which then leads to the need for even more cost cutting. In such a chaotic situation, there is no way but down.

There will inevitably come a time when the company will again need the energy and commitment of its employees, a time when the company will realize the truth of what its executives have always said but never really believed: that its people are its greatest assets. When that time comes, the companies that have played the cost-cutting layoff game will have a very difficult time winning back the trust and commitment necessary to restore productivity and growth.

15

*True perfection seems imperfect,
yet it is perfectly itself. . . .*

(from Chapter 45)

When you concoct an ideal for your employees, nothing will ever live up to it. Compared to the elusive ideal, you are assured of failure.

When the great awakening to quality swept American companies several years ago, many of them developed programs that incorporated the concept of "continuous improvement." This method is intended to empower people by giving them information that will help them make improvements in their jobs. It was a very successful development in those companies whose managers realized that the key lay not in measurements but in the commitment of employees to continuously improve their work. It was not so successful in companies that chose to drive their employees by close supervision. These companies imposed continuous improvement on their employees as just another technocratic way to assure compliance with productivity standards.

There are too many bosses for whom the good work of their employees is never good enough. They assume that every worker and every piece of work can be improved. "Nobody's perfect," they like to say, as if perfection were the goal. The wise leader, on the other hand, holds the more paradoxical assumption that every person and every piece of work are perfect—but there's still lots of room for improvement.

Judging employees by ideal standards that exist only in the mind condemns them to mediocrity and deprives them of the opportunity to be excellent. So set goals and standards of performance individually, with each person participating fully. The standards of performance should be a moral agreement, a covenant, between you and the employee. People who set their own standards will want to achieve more each year, whereas if you set the standards as a manager, it leaves them with no reason to want to improve; they simply wait for you to set the next year's goals.

The wise leader recognizes that acceptance is more important than empty comparisons, and that by accepting her employees' work and getting out of the way, she will be guiding them to even greater performance.

16

The ancient Masters
didn't try to educate the people,
but kindly taught them to not-know.

When they think that they know the answers,
people are difficult to guide.
When they know that they don't know,
people can find their own way. . . .

(from Chapter 65)

The most precious gift you can give to up-and-coming managers is to urge that they adopt an attitude of what Zen calls "don't-know mind." This is also called "beginner's mind." It is the mind that isn't limited by any ideas, the mind that is open to all possibilities. This is difficult to understand, and difficult to put into practice, yet it is the most creative space in the world. All the great works of science and art have come from letting go of preconceptions. Out of this mind has arisen everything from Newton's theory of gravity to Einstein's theory of relativity, Bach's work to Stravinsky's, Sappho's to Emily Dickinson's, Praxiteles' to Cézanne's.

There is no doubt that you, as a manager, will at some point become a mentor for new managers and leaders. Don't be confused by the idea of not-knowing. Resist the temptation to try to educate these up-and-coming people about how to do all the things you've learned to do over the years. Remember that the people you're mentoring are up-and-coming because they've proven that they're very good at doing what they do. They don't need more technical information, and they don't need to know how you used to do things.

If you tell them what to do, they'll try it your way if you're senior to them in the organization. If you're their boss, they'll definitely try it your way. But there are two problems with your way: (1) It may be wrong for this time and this place; and (2) It will deprive you and the company of their creativity and new ideas.

What they do need is a sense that questions are more important than answers and that whatever answers exist now are answers to old questions. These answers may not work for tomorrow's questions; changing circumstances will dictate different questions and answers. They need you to guide them in finding their own answers, regardless of what changes may come throughout their careers. Thus, your emphasis should not be on what to do but on how to be.

It is essential to realize that the Tao Te Ching is not praising ignorance. Chapter 1 of the Tao Te Ching refers to darkness as "the gateway to all understanding." This means that the wise leader sees through the conventional definitions of light as good and darkness as bad. He knows that creative people in any field have always recognized and honored the darkness, not as something negative but as part of their creative process.

This is more practical than it may sound at first. Surely you've said at one time or another, "I'll sleep on that problem," meaning not that you plan to procrastinate but that, rather than force a solution, you'll stop thinking about the problem and let your unconscious mind work on it. Often the solution will appear by itself, like magic.

In trying to understand "don't-know mind," reflect on

your own career. You know that some of your most profound insights or creative solutions have not resulted from
analysis but have just come to you, sometimes when you
weren't even thinking about them. Every experienced
manager can recall a time when answers came only after he
had stopped thinking about the problem, or had even
given up altogether.

There is a saying, popular in the 1970s and 1980s:
"Keep your eye on the things you can't see." It was quoted
often but probably not so often understood. Let's put it
now in the form of a Zen koan, an enigma that can't be
solved by the rational mind: "How will I know what I can't
see?" Answer: "You'll know it when you can't see it."

Can anyone see how a sale is made? You can analyze
and critique the information, the data, the sales calls, the
presentation, the follow-ups, the leave-withs, and so on,
but every experienced sales manager knows that none of
that makes the sale. A person does. One sales rep can make
a call, present the case, and the buyer says no, while
another sales rep can then make a call on the same buyer,
make the same case, and the buyer says yes. Why? No one
knows. The fact is that all we can do is put together a list of
the technical things most likely to work, then depend on
what we call "chemistry." The mystery of a successful sale
is one of those things we know is there but can't see.

The wise leader knows that mysteries can't be explained, but they can be used. By his example, he teaches
those around him to live in the open space that comes
from not-knowing.

—17—

All streams flow to the sea
because it is lower than they are.
Humility gives it its power.

If you want to govern the people,
you must place yourself below them.
If you want to lead the people,
you must learn how to follow them. . . .

(from Chapter 66)

This is one of the most profound leadership chapters in the Tao Te Ching. Here you are asked to abandon two additional dualisms that have always been at the heart of traditional business thinking: "lead or follow" and "above or below."

Most of our popular business mythology has evolved around images of the strong leader, out in front leading the company into the great marketplace wars. The Chrysler television commercial "Lead . . . or get out of the way" fully played into those images, with—who else?—the CEO of Chrysler himself sounding the charge.

We have been conditioned by many powerful images to think of the leader as always charismatic, the epitome of everything that everyone wants to be, the one who knows how to do anything. We make the leader into a cross between a God figure and a commanding general. Whether our image is of an Eisenhower or Patton, Roosevelt or Churchill or Kennedy, it is always someone who is a revered or feared—but always respected—commander.

So it seems heresy for the text to suggest that to become a wise leader, you must stand the whole notion of "lead or follow" on its head by being "back among" rather than out in front. But here's the reality: You can't lead people unless they are willing to follow you. To do that, you must inspire them to trust you with their very well-being, and in business, the well-being of your employees is in your care during most of their waking hours. The people will trust you if you can bring out their own sense of worth and creativity, and the only way to do this is to really know them and their abilities.

So in the beginning, and periodically throughout your leadership career, you must be willing to follow your employees, so that you can learn what to do in order to inspire them to follow you. You have to place yourself below the people in a way that lets you become familiar with their skills and strengths, needs and weaknesses. This requires more than looking through their records or giving a once-a-year appraisal; it requires staying in touch with them day to day and actively working to provide the resources they need, whether that's money, equipment, or your help in setting priorities and making decisions.

Being back among is a way of perceiving things more clearly; don't confuse it with such superficial gimmicks as management by walking about. Can you imagine the reaction of a junior employee who looks up and sees the big boss stick her head into his office and ask, "How are things going today?" There was one CEO who went so far as to have his secretary schedule a certain time three days a week when he would "walk about." It scared the hell out of people.

And don't think you can become just another one of the workers either. Everyone always knows who the boss is; you can't escape it. The issue is not about your visibility as the boss. It's about how you respond to it. Do you appear like someone wearing a crown and carrying a scepter, or do you take the role—in the late Robert Greenleaf's words—of the "servant leader"? It requires as much courage to be an enabler as to be a commander. But even in the process of empowering your employees, or being a resource, a "servant," you still can't abdicate the responsibility of leadership. You can delegate authority so that your people will act on their own, but you can't delegate the responsibility for the results of that action.

When you succeed in the discipline of being back among, when you learn to see the workplace as your employees see it, you gain a perspective that illuminates your view of the department or company. So many times, the big picture of an organization is dangerously distorted, because it is viewed only from the executive suite and doesn't receive the input of the employees closest to the product, the process, or the customers.

Because of your higher perspective and the way you were able to gain it—by being back among, rather than out in front—the effect of your leadership will be that no one feels oppressed. On the contrary, your employees will sense that you truly understand what needs to be done and how each of them can contribute.

One striking example makes the case: Several years ago, a senior manager of a plant that was about to be shut down and sold off organized his employees to join him in buying the business. It was in terrible condition. The equipment was dated, the market was soft, and there had been nothing but losses. But this manager and his employees mortgaged their houses, borrowed everything they could, and bought the place. They rebuilt it, and in a few years, it became profitable and began expanding. From the beginning of the new company, the manager, now CEO, decided that he would have a completely open operation, sharing all financial information every month, even with those employees who were not owners, making himself fully accessible to everyone, and keeping everyone informed about the condition of the business. "The more I tell the employees and the more they tell me," he explained, "the better we'll do. Besides, I didn't want to be one of those guys who leads the charge up the hill, then looks back to find no one following."

In addition to the courage it requires for you to go against the conventional leadership myth, you also must have humility to think of yourself as following your employees. And humility was probably not one of the characteristics you nurtured in order to achieve the position you now have. Humility certainly is not in anyone's business school curriculum.

Yet when you reach a certain point, the point at which you begin the move from management to leadership, it is the letting go of the ego needs of authority and control in favor of humility and service that will deliver you from the old competitive hero leader game and allow you to be effective by being fully available to everyone, above and below, leading and following.

— 18 —

When the Master governs, the people
are hardly aware that he exists. . . .

The Master doesn't talk, he acts.
When his work is done,
the people say, "Amazing:
we did it, all by ourselves!"

(from Chapter 17)

The top job in most large public companies has become a celebrity game in which the CEO spends more time with financial analysts than with employees or customers. He is a figure held in awe by the employees; not only are they aware that he exists, they'd *better* be.

This chapter is one of the best known and most quoted texts in the Tao Te Ching, yet its essential message of invisible leadership is antithetical to the way business leaders act today.

The wise leader realizes that the less his presence is felt, the more freedom the people will feel and the more they will be engaged by their work.

The idea of the invisible leader has particular application in today's workplace of self-managed teams, in which leadership emerges according to the project at hand. It is important, at the end of a project, for the team members to be less conscious of the leader than of their combined efforts. For this to happen, the top leaders of a company should establish the right environment; they should themselves model how it is to be. This means turning the organization chart upside down and considering themselves as members of the larger team. They should see themselves as resources for—and not bosses of—the people.

The concept of liberating people from your presence means investing in their training, so that their skills give them the confidence to accept greater responsibility. It also means that, in staying out of the way, you must bring your complete trust to the workplace.

Paradoxically, the best way to achieve invisibility is to always be available as a resource. When an employee has presented her ideas and made the case for a new project, don't say, "Report to me on this project every Monday." Instead ask, "How can I help?" When an employee admits that he made a mistake, don't ask, "What are you going to do about it?" Instead ask, "How can I help?" If your first question is "How can I help?" you open limitless possibilities.

And try these five useful questions in situations of planning, counseling, or even conflict:

- What do you think we should do?
- If you were in my position, what would you do now?
- If I could say exactly what you'd like to hear, what would it be?
- What do you really want me to do?

- If you could project the best possible outcome, the outcome you'd most like to see, what would it be?

If you can accept the role of leader without the lime-light, if you can trust the employees and quietly assure them that they have the resources to do their work, if you can be a resource yourself, then when your work is done, your employees will say—with a wonder and enthusiasm that will carry over into the rest of their lives—"Amazing! We did it! All by ourselves!"

Part II

Giving Up Control

19

. . . The Master does his job
and then stops.
He understands that the universe
is forever out of control,
and that trying to dominate events
goes against the current of the Tao. . . .

(from Chapter 30)

The faultiest assumption business people make is that they can be in control. Control is an illusion, and the quest for control creates endless mischief in the workplace.

Where does it come from, this compulsion to control? Organizationally, of course, it derives from the old command/control management model, which began in the church and became widespread in the military. But this only explains the structure that supports the desire to control. The real basis for it is the fear that something will go wrong and you'll be blamed and lose everything, just because you weren't in control.

The most frustrated managers in the world are those who spend their business lives trying to achieve control. Yet most of them would find it hard to explain what they're trying to control. They seem to believe that if things are done the way they, the managers, want them to be done, that's control. Or if the people behave on the job the way the managers want them to behave, that's control. Thus, many managers waste a lot of time on process and behavior, and are frustrated when the desired results are not achieved.

You can set up elaborate systems of work flow so that everything crosses your desk, you can review every plan and every line item in the budget, you can approve every trip proposal and scour every expense report, you can take your cell phone and computer on vacations so that the office will be at your fingertips at all times, you can do every single hiring and job assignment yourself, and you can make yourself the clearinghouse for every piece of information going in and out of your operation. But you still won't be in control; something will always happen that you didn't foresee.

There are a thousand uncontrollable things, from the state of the economy to the weather, that can affect your business results, either positively or negatively. You might respond, "All the more reason that I should try to control what I can." But if you can't control the outcome, what makes you think you can control the process?

The CEO of a large department store chain tells his managers, "If you can control anyone at all, you can control only a very few people—but you can influence an infinite number." Another CEO used to say, "We can't control profit, so let's not even talk about it. Profit is like breathing. Let's talk about what we need to do to keep the body healthy and thriving. If we do that, naturally we'll keep breathing."

Workplace behavior and performance are influenced by

compensation, by the physical environment, and by your ability to motivate people through your words and your example. This is what makes management an art and not a science. If it were possible to truly control processes and people, there would be no need for managers; computers could do the job.

You take the first big step toward management maturity when you realize that you are not in control, that, in fact, the world is out of control. Ask yourself, "What controls the stock market or the commodities market, what controls the economy, what controls consumer confidence?" Nothing you can be sure about. For instance, the chairman of the Fed may complain about "irrational exuberance" in the stock market, and the market will plunge. But did anything change in the companies' performance that day? Is there anything those CEOs could have done about it? Of course not. The market isn't and can't be under control. Otherwise why would economists be so shocked and why would the stock market swing so wildly when employment figures or consumer price index figures come in outside the "experts' " expectations?

So don't kid yourself about your ability to dominate events and circumstances. On the other hand, it's fair to ask, "If I just respond to the 'current of the Tao,' to conditions as they are, isn't that being wishy-washy?"

Fair question, but be careful how you define "wishy-washy." Contrary to the ethic of macho decisiveness, changing your mind is not weakness. The world is constantly changing, and your people are constantly changing. One senior manager says that, at any given time, twenty percent of her people are depressed or distracted, having health problems, getting engaged or married or divorced, having a baby, or just not focused that day. You need to recognize the changes, positive and negative, that affect the workplace and respond to them as skillfully as you can.

What is necessary is to be quick on your feet today and responsive to what the marketplace demands, while having powerful values that hold your culture and the harmony of the workplace together. Then be ready to change your mind tomorrow about particular strategies, plans, or agendas, if necessary. That's what the current of the Tao demands.

20

Fill your bowl to the brim
and it will spill.
Keep sharpening your knife
and it will blunt. . . .

Do your work, then step back.
The only path to serenity.

(from Chapter 9)

In striving for continuous improvement and higher productivity, you can push so hard for "more, bigger, faster" that you diminish your people and impede the results you most desire. You also diminish yourself and impede your own growth.

In the quest for the perfect schedule, we become obsessive instead of productive. We use all the marvelous tools of technology—laptops and cell phones, beepers and voice mail—but rather than saving time, they seduce us into taking on more. This compulsion to do more in less time has become epidemic in business, and you always hear the rationale that we're squeezing more out of our time because of these electronic tools. But are we? Perhaps we're just intrigued with the tools, so we come up with more ways to use them. Perhaps they have changed from tools to symbols of our self-importance: "If I'm out of touch, the world will collapse."

Busy-ness can be a form of laziness. With so many companies stressing the popular mantra "We have a bias toward action," business people begin to feel that success depends on doing something all the time. So they stay busy. But in doing so, they often use their busy-ness as a substitute for creative thinking, or they hide behind how busy they are. In other words, they're so involved with the image of how busy they are that they don't really get anything done. Surely you know a manager who rushes from place to place with his coffee cup or a manila folder, occasionally stopping to take a deep breath at his assistant's desk, slapping his head in frustration, striding purposefully off to the next big meeting. How many times have you heard (or said), "I don't even have time to think about that problem because of all the meetings, phone calls, and correspondence." Or, "Strategic thinking? Hell, I don't have time to put out today's brushfires, never mind three years from now."

Has the quality of our work improved? Has the quality of our lives improved? When you live with a squeeze-it-in mentality—squeeze in one more phone call from the car, squeeze in one more memo on the laptop before the plane lands, squeeze in one more meeting when you'd just be sitting in traffic trying to get home—you rob yourself of any time to reflect on your work and life. You sacrifice private time to relax, to be entertained, to enjoy the freedom of having nothing to do. It was a dramatic symbol of this perversion when, at the Cannes Film Festival, there were announcements before every film urging members of the audience to turn off their beepers and cell phones.

More is not necessarily better. Often more can be worse. The wise leader knows when to forge ahead and when to step back. That is what makes her a source of strength and sanity for everyone around her.

— 21 —

If you want to be a great leader,
you must learn to follow the Tao.
Stop trying to control.
Let go of fixed plans and concepts,
and the world will govern itself.

The more prohibitions you have,
the less virtuous people will be. . . .

(from Chapter 57)

The more rules you make, the less people will do things on their own and the more effort they will put into circumventing your rules. Most companies operate on the principle that if employees are given half a chance they'll do something wrong. A culture of prohibition derives from two common management shortcomings: the compulsion to control and the desire to manage people in groups rather than one at a time. Typically, if an employee is doing something that is counterproductive, the manager will avoid confronting the employee directly and will instead send a memo or write a policy prohibiting everyone from doing what only one employee is doing.

Most people will do the right thing when left to use their own judgment. And most of the time, an appeal to common sense will suffice. In one sales and marketing company, it became clear that a pattern of excessive attendance at trade shows had developed over the years. Too many people from the company were spending too much time and money covering the trade shows. The attendance list had grown as the company had prospered and more people were hired. No one had ever questioned the number.

As a remedy, the senior vice president of sales might have said to his department heads, "Listen, folks, we have over fifty people attending the such-and-such show at a cost of almost a hundred thousand dollars, twice a year. Figure out a way to cut this down and still get the show covered." That's it. It would have been done as a matter of common sense and good planning.

Instead, the senior VP devised a complicated formula for determining who should attend trade shows, and when. In addition, he required trip and call reports and a narrative of each day's activities. The result was a burdensome chore for the salespeople and a chore for the VP's staff in reviewing and filing all this paperwork. It took all flexibility out of the selection process, which in turn stimulated a lot of creative attempts to qualify for attendance.

The company should state clearly that it will operate within the letter and the spirit of the law, and according to the highest moral standards. Nothing more needs to be said. Rules should be limited to three categories: (1) what the law requires and what procedures the company has instituted in order to comply with the law; (2) policies that guide people in techniques or procedures about work flow and efficiency, operational and accountability matters, purchasing, budgeting, approvals, and so on (some of which is connected to legal compliance); (3) policies and guidelines about hiring, appraisals and evaluations, compensation (some of which is also connected to legal compliance)—and of course, there should be manuals and other explicit employee materials explaining benefits.

It's not the policies listed above that cause the problems; it's the ad hoc policies of individual departments. A manager might say, "I think too many people are surfing the Internet instead of doing their jobs. Let's have a policy against that." This assumes that if the employee is doing anything not specifically in the job description, he must not be working. In earlier days, a favorite target was talk sessions at the watercooler. And some managers still mentally clock their employees in and out for lunch breaks.

But what's the appropriate way to evaluate work? By results or by appearances? Who says that surfing the Net can't be a productive way to get good ideas? Who says that playing computer games for a while isn't better for relaxation than an approved coffee break? Who really knows the source of people's creativity? If you focus on appearances instead of results, you are creating an environment in which people invest their energy in appearances rather than results. If your employees are achieving good results and are behaving with respect for one another, so what if they aren't doing it according to the rules?

The more you try to tell people exactly how to do their work, the less they'll bring their creativity to it. The more you try to control, the less influence you'll have. The wise leader knows that nothing good can be compelled from people; it can only be elicited from them. By letting go of the need for control, both he and the employees are liberated from the tyranny of expectation, and the workplace becomes a center of creativity, commitment, passion, and productive activity.

—22—

Governing a large country
is like frying a small fish.
You spoil it with too much poking.

Center your country in the Tao
and evil will have no power.
Not that it isn't there,
but you'll be able to step out of its way.

Give evil nothing to oppose
and it will disappear by itself.

(Chapter 60)

When a manager looks over employees' shoulders, they begin to feel repressed. No matter how well they do their jobs, they know they'll be criticized, so they don't do their best work. Repression provokes resentment, and there is nothing more likely to spoil the workplace environment. These powerful feelings can move people to do the wrong thing, because they convince themselves that they are entitled to do whatever they can to feel less repressed or to feel they have extracted some retribution.

People have the capacity to do great work, and most people want to be honest and productive—but they also have the capacity to justify dishonest and counterproductive things. This could take the relatively benign form of pilfering office supplies, but it could also take more destructive forms. Your employees are just as smart about how not to get things done as they are about how to get things done, and most managers would be hard put to quickly determine when a project has been undermined by neglect or production has been deliberately slowed down.

How people choose to behave depends on how they are led. If a company finds no value in being a place in which the employees can express the best of who they are through their work, then its managers are more likely to express their power through exploitation and manipulation of the employees.

But if a company is centered in the Tao—if it holds the space in which people can be honest and do great work without fear of micromanagement, harsh criticism, or unreasonable demands—its managers will see themselves as resources for the people. They know that intelligent non-interference is the best way to avoid major difficulties in the workplace. Intelligent non-interference is for a company what good dietary habits and preventive medicine are for the body: you step out of the way of serious problems even before they arise.

. . . The world is sacred.
It can't be improved.
If you tamper with it, you'll ruin it.
If you treat it like an object, you'll lose it. . . .

(from Chapter 29)

The desire to improve your business is good, but giving in to the temptation to tamper can ruin things. Change is not necessarily improvement. Much of what passes for change these days is simple tampering. Why? Because the changes are without clear purpose and are addressed to the business as object rather than the business as an organic, living-and-breathing community of people. Many of the management fads have been imposed by CEOs on businesses seemingly without regard for whether the particular system is appropriate for the business. Total Quality Management is a good example. Enterprises as diverse as manufacturing plants, universities, and hospitals jumped into TQM a few years ago, and only later did many of them determine that TQM was not just another analytical system to be pushed down the throats of the employees, but instead required a virtual revolution in interpersonal relationships and organization within the company. In other words,

TQM depends entirely on the involvement of the com-munity of workers.

Some companies, with great fanfare, will embrace these kinds of management fads *du jour*, then when the new thing doesn't produce a quick miracle, they will aban-don it for something else. Some companies, with an eye on short-term stock price improvement, will change manage-ment teams regularly. Other companies, without real study or evaluation, will shut down longtime service de-partments and outsource those services, often at no cost savings whatsoever and with a lower quality result.

And in the most damaging tampering of all, some managers will create substantial turnover, saying, "We need better people around here." They look for flaws in everyone's work. They become convinced that other com-panies have better people, and that if they could just find better people they'd get better results. So they develop a pattern of hiring a golden boy to fix everything, then becoming disillusioned that he's only human after all. They change job assignments or assign one person to take over the duties of another person, who then feels unvalued and leaves. There was a midwestern publisher of consumer magazines whose senior management became convinced that the only good, aggressive publishing managers were in New York. It's an old story: The New York people who were brought in weren't miracle workers. They were no more competent than the midwesterners, plus they didn't want to live in the Midwest. More turnover.

Your people are sacred. Their basic humanity can't be improved upon; it transcends their jobs, it is part of who they are as human beings. Management itself is a calling, a sacred trust in which the well-being of other people is put into your care during most of their waking hours. You can do things to influence habits, to build an atmosphere in which people are more trusting of one another and more cooperative. You can create an environment in which they can do better and more productive work. You can train them in the technical and administrative aspects that are crucial to any job. You can provide clarity about what is to be done. You can give people the resources they need. And you can be a resource yourself. So you can improve their work, but you can't improve the people.

The wise leader knows when it's time for change and when it's not, because she understands that change is beyond her control. She is patient and remains so tuned in to everything affecting her business that she knows when all things are ready and it's time to move.

— 24 —

. . . *The Master trusts people who are*
   trustworthy.
She also trusts people who aren't trustworthy.
This is true trust.

The Master's mind is like space.
People don't understand her.
They look to her and wait.
She treats them like her own children.

(from Chapter 49)

Trust is like love. Either it's unconditional or it's not trust. If you say, "I'll trust the people who prove to me they can be trusted," you're saying, "I'm not a trustful person and I don't really trust anyone." Once you set conditions on your trust, you'll waste a lot of time and energy deciding whom you can trust and whom you can't. You should trust everyone you work with, the managers above you as well as your employees. The only other choice is to begin by trusting no one, and by making everyone prove his worthiness to you. That choice leads to fruitless relationships, creates poor morale and low productivity, and retards your own growth as a leader.

Start with the attitude that people want to do a good job and that they will if you trust them to. Of course, not everyone wants to do a good job and not everyone can accept trust. But try not to filter this through your ego, which will cause you to think of an employee's untrustworthiness as a personal betrayal. This will only lead you into a distrustful attitude in order to protect yourself from the pain of betrayal. Just accept the fact that during your career there will be people who will lie to you and who will take advantage of your good will, but realize that ultimately they damage themselves, not you. And don't bother trying to figure out who they are; just give them time, and 'they'll commit a fireable offense. Meanwhile you will not have punished all your good people by setting up a culture of prohibition and distrust. If you do set up such a culture, it will just take that much longer for the untrustworthy people to surface.

Be sure you understand the definition of trust. Some managers may put it this way: "There are situations in which I just can't trust a certain salesperson to handle a presentation alone because he's not ready. What then?" This question is not about trust, it's about competence, though we frequently use "trust" in this context. Trust has to do with integrity, not competence. You may indeed have employees who don't yet have the experience or training to handle certain assignments, but assigning a more experienced person to help, or helping them yourself, does not show a lack of trust.

But when it comes to matters of integrity—of people doing what they say they'll do and behaving with honesty and fair dealing—don't withhold your trust. Your trust in others creates others' trust in you.

You may ask, "Should I just ignore people who I know can't be trusted? Should I trust them anyway? Shouldn't I take corrective action when someone betrays my trust?"

These are valid questions, because the leader must be

respectful of the group, and she knows that the untrust-worthiness of one can impose a great injustice on the rest of the group. There are mistakes and there are crimes; mistakes can be corrected, crimes must be punished. Be careful not to criminalize a mistake. If an employee mis-handles money by spending too much on an airline ticket or by having a lavish meal on the expense account, don't punish him as if he were an embezzler.

The wise leader knows how to set limits *within* the context of trust. Just as you can say no to your children, with love, as a help to them, you can critique an employee's mistakes of judgment while affirming his capacity for trustworthiness.

These are difficult challenges for leaders, but the reality is that you can only model values, you can't imbue people with them. You can hope they'll pick them up, but you can't force them to. You can't control another person's behavior, but you can engage every situation with an atti-tude of trust, because you realize that all people have the *capacity* to be trustworthy, even though they may not yet have arrived at that point. You can make a person feel so trusted and valued that he will respond by being trustwor-thy and valuable.

And if he doesn't respond in this way, fire him. Even in firing a person, don't give up on him altogether. True to your values, you can still affirm his capacity for trust-worthiness while keeping your heart open to him and conveying your sense of sadness and loss. The way you fire him may be, even if he isn't conscious of it, one of the greatest gifts he ever receives.

The Tao Te Ching recognizes that if you lead in this way, many employees will not understand and will not easily accept what you are trying to accomplish. But don't let that affect you. Keep a clear and open mind, and know that your best choice is to continue to treat all people with respect and to trust them without restraint. In other words, you should give them the patient support and encouragement you would give your own children.

25

When a country obtains great power,
it becomes like the sea:
all streams run downward into it.
The more powerful it grows,
the greater the need for humility.
Humility means trusting the Tao,
thus never needing to be defensive.

A great nation is like a great man:
When he makes a mistake, he realizes it.
Having realized it, he admits it.
Having admitted it, he corrects it. . . .

(from Chapter 61)

The bigger a company gets, the more complacent and arrogant it usually becomes. Despite their talk about innovation and change, bureaucracies perpetuate themselves, and their managers insist on rigid compliance with company rules. The case histories of failed companies, or of companies that have fallen into crisis, inevitably tell of management that refused to question its own actions, could not admit the possibility of mistakes, and circled the wagons in the face of criticism.

Great leaders, and thus great companies, realize that the more power and influence they gain, the more humble they need to be. They admit their mistakes and create opportunities for their critics to be heard. And great leaders accept criticism gracefully. This is not true of most large companies, whose usual, arrogant response to criticism is to gear up their public relations defense machines. Obvious examples are the *Exxon Valdez* accident, allegations of the fire vulnerability of GM pickup trucks, similar accusations in the seventies about Ford Pinto gas tanks, the Audi transmission malfunctions, and the Dow breast implant lawsuits.

Great leaders also recognize that internal criticism is valuable, but criticism that arises when there's no permission for criticism can lead to scapegoating. Whereas ordinary managers hear criticism as a personal attack requiring a harsh response, great leaders create a culture in which honest criticism is welcome, is not thought of as condemnation, and is valued as a means of improvement. Good companies create forums for self-appraisal. There is no underground of information control, no shooting the messenger who brings the bad news. Instead they talk about what happened and what to do next time. Rather than castigating the person who made the mistake, great leaders make them part of the solution.

The military is better at this than business is. The military may have trouble communicating to the public at large, but they have great systems for debriefing operations. They review everything about a mission to determine what was done well and what was done poorly. If someone made a mistake, does that person need more training? If it's a widespread mistake, does the unit need more training? The reason the military is so intentional about this process is that the stakes are so high: life and death.

The wise leader's ease with his own mistakes gives permission for everyone to admit *their* mistakes. It creates an atmosphere in which mistakes are freely admitted, most often before they became major problems, since there is virtually no fear of retribution. When an employee at a large New York media company was trying to close a deal on an acquisition, the CEO balked at the price, even though to the employee it seemed a bargain. The acquisition was made by another company, and she walked away mystified. The next day the CEO called to apologize for blowing it. He had been given incorrect information about what the acquisition was worth. Had he known the real value, he said, he would have jumped at the deal. The employee got off the phone with an enormously increased respect for her boss, much more at ease with the prospect of making her own mistakes, and inspired to work even harder.

26

Failure is an opportunity.
If you blame someone else,
there is no end to the blame.

Therefore the Master
fulfills her own obligations
and corrects her own mistakes. . . .

(from Chapter 79)

I n grand gestures toward empowerment, senior corporate managers are fond of telling their employees, "We encourage risk, and we reward mistakes. After all, mistakes are opportunities to learn." But just let something go wrong in their division or group—an unsuccessful product introduction or a promotion that fails and causes a loss of market share—and those same senior managers inevitably look for someone to blame. They write ass-covering memos and they fire people just to look as if they're handling the problem.

So employees don't believe that empowerment is real, and neither do middle and lower-level managers. "Make a mistake," they say to one another, "and you're outta here."

There's a lot of fear about failure and mistakes on the job, because there's a lot of scapegoating. Senior executives point fingers at middle managers, who point fingers at supervisors, who point fingers at employees, who point fingers at "management" because "management can't make up their minds" or "they should have seen that problem coming a mile away" or "they didn't give us what we needed to do the job." Scapegoating begets scapegoating.

The biggest problem with mistakes is that people let themselves *become* the mistake. They negate their own identity and take on the identity of the mistake itself. They think of themselves as The Person Who Made The Mistake, so everyone else thinks of them that way. But the first step toward a healthier sense of self-worth is to recognize that you don't have to become the mistake. In the same way that you're more than your job, you and your job are more than the mistake. It's hard for people to realize that mistakes are part of work and growth and innovation. If you're not making mistakes, you're not growing. Anyone good at product development would never have been able to introduce successful new products if she hadn't also had a few flops. Mistakes are normal and necessary in business.

The wise leader, because she fully accepts who she is, does what she thinks is right and does what she says she'll do. This is called integrity. And when she makes mistakes, she sees them for what they are, moves to correct them, and always claims full responsibility for them. This is called maturity.

— 27 —

In the pursuit of knowledge,
every day something is added.
In the practice of the Tao,
every day something is dropped.
Less and less do you need to force things,
until finally you arrive at non-action.
When nothing is done,
nothing is left undone. . . .

(from Chapter 48)

At one point in the writing of this book, we considered calling it *Doing Nothing, Leaving Nothing Undone*. On the positive side, this title would have accurately encapsulated the wisdom of the Tao Te Ching, and because business people are so obsessed with doing things, the apparent contradiction within the title might also have intrigued them. On the other hand, precisely because business people are so obsessed with doing things, they might very well have dismissed a book with this title as some sort of off-the-wall New Age nonsense. Yet the attitude of doing nothing and leaving nothing undone is the essence of this chapter.

Before you ask, "Hell, if I didn't do this, how would it get done?" first ask, "Does this really need to be done? What am I doing that's not necessary?" Managers usually avoid those questions, because they're afraid that much of what they do really isn't necessary and they're not comfortable with *not* being constantly busy. Everyone needs time to think, but most managers complain that there's no time for thinking. This is because business people have become conditioned to the belief that busy-ness denotes competence. They distrust the concept of downtime, and they distrust silence, the most fertile medium for creativity and vision.

So stop kidding yourself that you have to be doing something all the time in order to be a wise leader. Give not-doing a chance. Not-doing isn't the same as idleness or passivity. Wise leaders know how to delegate authority as well as tasks, without abandoning responsibility and accountability. Delegating is another way of dropping something. It means you let something go so that something greater can be done.

If you can delegate without feeling that you're giving up your hands-on connection with the work, and if you use the time you gain for creative thinking, you may end up looking as if you're not doing very much.

But you may be amazed that nothing is left undone.

Part III

Motivation

28

Success is as dangerous as failure.
Hope is as hollow as fear. . . .

See the world as your self.
Have faith in the way things are. . . .

(from Chapter 13)

I t probably sounds ridiculous to say that success is as dangerous as failure. Achieving professional status and income, which in turn give us economic flexibility, position, and influence in our communities, seems obviously preferable to a life of worrying about money, struggling to make ends meet, and never having big houses, fancy cars, club memberships, and extravagant vacations.

But suppose that you do "succeed," that you become a senior vice president or a CEO, that you get those promotions, bonuses, stock options. The danger is not in achieving these things as such; it's in using them as the standard for measuring yourself and in making them the reason you live and work. When this happens, your work loses its true meaning. At that point, the preoccupation with success and its symbols replaces the passion for your work, distracts you from your vision, and becomes dangerous for your business. You become so protective of what you have, and of what you still want to get, that you stop taking the creative risks that made you "successful" in the first place, and you begin to clamp down on your employees so that they won't take risks either.

Once you even use the words *success* and *failure,* once you think of yourself as having succeeded or having failed, you're in danger. Success and failure are only what you think you've done. They don't exist except in the abstract. There are two groups of people who end up unhappy. The first group is made up of people who set personal goals regarding position, power, and money, and don't attain those goals. The second group is made up of those who set personal goals regarding position, power, and money, and do attain those goals. The first group asks, "Where is it?" and the second group asks, "Is this it?" The people in the first group are preoccupied with what they don't have and think themselves failures for not having those things. Those in the second group are always trying to convince themselves that they're successful, because they've discovered that the amount of money and power that define success keeps racheting upward. What the groups have in common is that they want more of whatever it is they don't have.

In both cases, they are focused outward, toward what society has established as the definition of success and failure. The very acceptance of those labels means that you're not living in the present. Worse yet, you condemn yourself to be forever preoccupied with what you have or haven't done and what you are or aren't going to do. This is a great danger to your psychological and spiritual well-being, because, by definition, you can never have enough or do enough to satisfy yourself. You're *always* on the way up or on the way down. You live in a state of anticipation and frustration because you can never arrive.

The true risk of success is the risk of becoming unbalanced and ungrounded, of letting the short-term symbols of achievement become so compelling that you are willing to compromise or distort your values. How much time do you spend after business hours thinking about your work? How present and available are you to your spouse and children? When you are with them, are you fully with them? How satisfied are they with the amount and quality of the time you spend with them? If you've answered the first question "a lot," and the other questions "not much" or "not very," then success has become dangerous indeed.

What, then, is the meaning of success? Can the downsized worker or the manager passed over for promotion be as successful as someone who has not been laid off or who got the promotion? The danger lies in the way you think about it. There's no question that downsizing has caused much pain and fear among employees, yet today's small-business world has been reinvigorated by people who, having been downsized, decided to start their own businesses. They accepted things as they were and created new circumstances for themselves, because they dropped the baggage of having failed.

The preoccupation with success and failure means that you can never fully be in the present, that you can't enjoy the way things are because your attention is always on how things are not or will be or should be. It is in this regard that the text connects hope, fear, success, and failure.

Success is the other side of failure; hope is the other side of fear. They all embody the same attitude of focusing on the past or the future, and they keep you from bringing all of yourself—your energy, creativity, talent, and vision—to whatever is there for you today.

29

. . . The wise leader embodies
the virtue of non-competition.
Not that she doesn't love to compete,
but she does it in the spirit of play.
In this she is like a child
and in harmony with the Tao.

(from Chapter 68)

Wise leaders work to discourage rather than affirm destructive competition among individual employees within the company. Two things lead to this kind of competitiveness: the people themselves who think of it that way and management systems that put people in competition for jobs. You can deal with the first by doing away with the second. You can't keep some people from competing; they arrive in your company conditioned to compete, by everything from sports to previous employment experiences. Competitive people think that when a co-worker has succeeded, it means that they themselves have failed. It's not unusual for the person who's been passed over to resign or start looking for another job, thinking he must do so to save face. It's this mindset that keeps your company from being a true community.

So let people know immediately that there's no reward for competing with their fellow workers. Walk the talk of creating teams and communities and encouraging cross-functional work. Set up bonuses for teams. In several companies, there are team bonuses for sales groups that make their goals. These bonuses include everyone in the group, support people as well as salespeople, but are in addition to individual incentive plans. The incentive plans assure that the top producers are rewarded well, and the team plans break down the elitism by doing away with a culture of "haves" and "have-nots."

Of course, you encourage positive behaviors in everything you say, but money is a great reinforcer. The way to avoid destructive behavior is to not reward it, and the way to encourage positive behavior is to reward it. Simple. This builds a culture in which everyone performs for the good of the enterprise, and everyone understands that you don't have to be better, you just have to be good.

Someone who has begun to embody the virtue of non-competition might support and celebrate a colleague who received a promotion. He might feel a twinge of envy at first, but if he knows that the promotion is well deserved and good for the company, the bruise to his ego soon disappears and he returns to his work with renewed enthusiasm.

"But what if the promotion is *not* well deserved?" you might ask. "It's easier said than done to free myself of labels and work with enthusiasm." True, and if you really feel the company promotes unqualified people, you may have to prepare yourself to work somewhere else. The key is to ask, "Why am I reacting this way? Is it because I feel insulted, or do I feel that this promotion will injure the company? Do I want to stay and help this company through the next stage, or do I think it will be an unhealthy and unproductive place for me?" This process still transcends destructive competitive thinking.

The way a leader deals with competition will allow employees to frame things in this more helpful way. She encourages people to support and care for one another. The spirit of play makes competition, when it occurs, into something invigorating and cohesive, which works for the good of the whole company.

— 30 —

Express yourself completely,
then keep quiet. . . .

Open yourself to the Tao,
then trust your natural responses;
and everything will fall into place.

(from Chapter 23)

What happens when you're really angry at work? Should you bottle it up? Should you vent it? What's the most effective way of expressing your anger?

Shouting isn't the answer. Sometimes if managers feel personally betrayed when a mistake is made or their advice isn't heeded, they respond with verbal abuse. Rather than say, "I'm upset that the competition underpriced us and got that business," they spray their frustration at everyone around them.

You can begin to answer these questions by examining whether you're trying to communicate that you are angry or whether you're trying to intimidate. Good communication is never abusive.

It *is* difficult to deal with the rush of adrenaline you feel when someone has done something utterly wrongheaded. One senior manager who is a strong advocate of the principles contained in the Tao Te Ching nonetheless felt her temperature rise during a budget review meeting when she discovered an unexpected, unacceptable item. There was no explanation. There it was. Surprise! At one time or another, every manager faces a situation like this, and the only thing to do in that instant is . . . nothing. That's exactly what this manager did. She lowered her head and sat quietly until the adrenaline rush passed, then she expressed her anger directly at the problem rather than shouting down another human being.

If you're honestly trying to communicate that you're angry, by all means express it openly: "John, this mistake made me very angry. In fact, I'm having trouble containing myself because what you did seems so uncalled-for." That's enough. It's very different from yelling, "You stupid asshole, how could you do such a thing?"

It's okay to be angry. There will be disappointments and they need to be expressed. But if you do it in a way that shuts down communication, you have lost the opportunity to learn from those disappointments, because everyone around you will be paralyzed. Even discovering a massive budget error can become an opportunity for the employee to grow by helping to solve the problem he created, and for the community to bond by seeing how openly the mistake was handled. You don't need dramatic gestures to get your point across. You only need to be genuine. If all your expressions are authentic, then you are freeing those around you to work fearlessly.

31

. . . There is no greater misfortune
than underestimating your enemy.
Underestimating your enemy
means thinking that he is an enemy. . . .

When two great forces oppose each other,
the victory will go
to the one that knows how to yield.

(from Chapter 69)

It is much more helpful to think of your competitor as your opponent rather than your enemy. Once you frame things as "them against me," once you divide the world into friends and enemies, once you start reacting defensively to what your enemies do, you become an enemy yourself: an enemy to your enemies and an enemy to your own peace of mind. While this text is specifically written to avoid force in military situations, it is useful as well in avoiding unnecessary confrontations.

In the martial arts, there is great emphasis on using the energy of your opponent in defending yourself. In self-defense or in competitive business situations, you weaken your strategic position if you act only in the attack mode. By remaining fluid enough to simply step back from a situation, or step aside, you are capable of responding creatively to many different situations.

Recently, one company in a high-visibility industry began to reduce prices drastically, undercutting everyone else. The response of most competitors was anger: "How the hell can they do that? What are they trying to do, ruin us all, destroy the industry?" Naturally, they also went on the attack and cut prices even more. And so on.

But one company took advantage of all the excitement the price war had stirred up to do something different. It cut prices modestly, then offered several value-added services, including seminars for its customers' salespeople, cross-promotional opportunities with other companies, and special co-op advertising deals. All these added cost, of course, but it didn't cost as much as simply cutting prices would have. In addition, when the war was over, the company had improved its market share and was able to raise its prices disproportionately, because its customers perceived that they were getting so much more through the value-added programs. When all was said and done, this company had benefited greatly from using the energy the competitor had generated.

If you don't remain agile, you'll become like many large corporations that have suffered competitively because their own momentum was so great and so reinforced by hidebound policies that restricted people's creativity. Some obvious examples are IBM, AT&T, and General Motors; there are many more.

The usual macho business mind equates yielding with losing; to someone with an insecure ego, it feels like an intolerable surrender of control. But all natural things know how and when to yield. A branch will bend rather than break as an intelligent response to a strong wind. A palm tree will bend all the way to the ground in a hurricane, then afterward snap back up, perfectly straight. Yielding can also be the equivalent of winning, as the text says. The great advantage of knowing how to yield is that even in your victory, your opponent—business competitor, ambitious colleague, or spouse—won't feel defeated.

32

When a country is in harmony with the Tao,
the factories make trucks and tractors.
When a country goes counter to the Tao,
warheads are stockpiled outside the cities.

There is no greater illusion than fear,
no greater wrong than preparing to defend
  yourself,
no greater misfortune than having an enemy.

Whoever can see through all fear
will always be safe.

(Chapter 46)

A lot has been written about business as war. Business people have been offered Sun-tzu's *The Art of War* and von Clausewitz's treatises on strategy as guidelines for doing business.

But business is not war. Nothing about it resembles war. Going after a larger market share to the detriment of your competitor's market share isn't war. Pricing below a competitor's price isn't war. And if a business does take market share from another business, that doesn't equal winning on the battlefield.

It has become popular to motivate employees by talking about "shooting the competition," "taking no prisoners," and even "bayoneting the wounded." All this war imagery has one intent: to express hostility. Yet an attitude of hostility toward other companies wastes a lot of energy. It's not helpful for an industry and not healthy for its people. Often you'll work with the same people in an industry for a long time, so to demonize them when they're with a competitor is senseless. Whatever your industry, you need to have an attitude of stewardship. If an industry isn't healthy, your company won't be healthy either.

No one can point to any useful business purpose that an attitude of hostility toward the competition has ever accomplished. And think of how it distracts, rather than focuses, the people. In one company, it became the norm for a salesperson to say, "Well, we didn't get the business but those sons-a-bitches at XYZ didn't get it either." The salespeople became so caught up in the hostility that they began to consider it a success if the competition didn't succeed, rather than concentrating on doing their part to assure their own company's success.

Your competitors are not your enemies. In fact, you share far more similarities than dissimilarities with them. An enlightened business leader knows that a good competitor helps focus the market and spread positive messages about your industry. Several years ago, a media company started a magazine appealing to a special group of young readers. It was a difficult start-up because the advertising customers couldn't make the magazine fit with anything else being published. Then another media company started a magazine in competition. Rather than saying, "Why would they do that when we're having trouble breaking even?" the publisher of the first magazine said, "I welcome the competition. They'll help convince the advertising clients that this really is a viable market of readers. It should help open up some ad dollars. When that happens, we can put our sales energy into presenting our product rather than defining the market."

Clearly, there is confidential and proprietary information that should not be shared; there are legal prohibitions against collusion; and there is always an appropriate effort to gain a marketplace advantage. Fair enough. But there are also activities to be shared in an industry's best interest, such concerns as government regulation, pending legislation, a need to train and educate workers, cooperation in development of infrastructure, or products that are too capital intensive for one company alone.

Unfortunately, it seems that American business in recent years has hatched a brood of gunslinger CEOs who see their aggressive public stances as strong signals to stock analysts, thus as beneficial to stock prices. Who knows if this is true in the short term, but it is certainly not beneficial to the company in the long term. Phil Jackson, coach of the champion Chicago Bulls, warns his team that while winning is great, it should never come at the expense of the other team's dignity. A humiliating victory will only ignite hostility in the other team, meaning a dirtier game next time, likely to take out key players through fouls and injuries.

Several years ago, a major toothpaste maker learned that a competitor was about to introduce a competitive cavity-fighting product in the family-dentifrice market. With this piece of industrial espionage in hand, the product manager for the major brand decided to offer their giant, family-size toothpaste in a national buy-one-and-get-another-for-one-cent promotion. His explanation: "We'll kick those bastards by taking millions of families out of the dentifrice market just as their new product hits the shelves. It'll take them another month to begin to get off the ground." The promotion worked, it kept the competitor's product from gaining market share for at least another month—but, of course, it kept those millions of families from buying *anybody's* toothpaste during that period and cost everybody a lot of money. Was it worth it? In dollars and cents, absolutely not, because the one-cent sale ate up that period's profits. And in the longer term, the competitor was simply delayed, not deterred, from entering the market. But the product manager was as smug as he could be.

People who view their professions as a world of hostile competition often do it because they *require* enemies for comparison. Without a reference point of who they are *not,* they don't know who they are. These managers may indeed become "successful," but in the process they create a world of conflict in which employees are encouraged to demonize competitors and celebrate their misfortune, rather than realize that the demise of one business in an industry creates doubts about the industry itself—by media, by investors, perhaps by government—and thus weakens everyone in the industry. Beyond business concerns, no decent person, knowing how much misery is involved, should be happy when a company fails.

People who think of business as war, and then develop strategies and tactics as if they were going into battle, create an unreal world of fear for themselves and their employees. And what are they left with? Whether they win or lose, their minds become battlefields strewn with corpses.

Business people who see through all this as simply a concoction, and an irrelevant one at that, will be able to concentrate on doing their business with civility and courtesy. When you sincerely wish others well, most people will be aware of your intention, and will wish you well in return. Thus, in acting courteously, you contribute to a legacy of peace not only for your employees but also for the world.

33

If you overesteem great men,
people become powerless.
If you overvalue possessions,
people begin to steal.

. . . The Master leads
by emptying people's minds
and filling their cores,
by weakening their ambition
and toughening their resolve. . . .

(from Chapter 3)

Since only a few people are ever going to get a lot of power and money, emphasizing power and money guarantees frustration and a sense of failure for everyone else. When recognition and reward are available to only the few, the great majority will feel unrecognized and unrewarded. When managers establish that the value system of the workplace emphasizes money and status, they undermine the internal rewards of good work.

The wise leader doesn't argue against increases in authority and compensation—promotions and raises—as rewards for good work, but he also understands that preoccupation with power and money undermines the very soul of an organization. Once the emphasis is put on the rewards, instead of on the work itself, then everyone from CEO to line worker begins to care only about rewards.

This is a prescription for disaster. People who get power will cling to it, and everyone else will feel powerless. People in power will create ways to reward themselves out of all proportion to other employees, thus creating an economic class structure within an organization. Once the employees perceive that the workplace culture is one of haves and have-nots, the company is headed for disruption. This may come simply as resentment that undermines commitment to the job at hand, or it may take a more serious form. Too many of today's business leaders seem not to have a sense of history, seem not to recognize that whenever workers feel repressed they find ways to express their frustration. Recent events clearly indicate a coming period of management/labor conflict including walkouts and strikes—a disaster for many American businesses—yet the downsizings and inflated executive pay continue unabated, as if boards of directors and senior executives can't grasp the connection between an economic class-system and unhappy employees.

Less disruptive but still of concern is the matter of perks, which people in power use to further enhance their own sense of prestige. Everyone seeks fairness, so when employees see the few at the top place great value on perks, employees feel justified in finding ways to create perks for themselves: a longer lunch break, an increase in sick days, a few bucks here or there on an expense account, some software for the home computer, even that old standby, office supplies.

The Tao Te Ching observes that the wise leader liberates employees, at all levels, by emptying their minds of these trivialities and filling them with a passion for substance. This means creating rewards that are commensurate with the real contribution to an overall effort—paying for performance and not according to traditional hierarchy systems of compensation. (For instance, could an individual salesperson produce such a sales volume that she is paid more than the VP of sales? Absolutely.) And it means doing away with silly perks and privileges.

Most of the things that contribute only to executives' and employees' sense of prestige have been created in the service of ambition. To be thought of as ambitious in business is generally considered a compliment. Yet in this chapter, the Tao Te Ching says that ambition is not a desirable trait, that it must be weakened. The text makes a clear distinction between ambition and resolve: *ambition* is an ego word, whereas *resolve* is the long-term commitment to achievement which, of course, is the most powerful asset a company can have. This commitment depends on everyone's own internal reward system. How do you think of yourself? How do you find identity outside your work? How essential to your well-being are the things you own?

The wise leader keeps people focused on the work itself and its long-term purpose, thus he weakens employees' short-term ambition to win and toughens their long-term resolve to create what is excellent in itself and valuable for the customers and the community at large.

Part IV

Creating a Community That Works

34

Every being in the universe
is an expression of the Tao.
It springs into existence,
unconscious, perfect, free,
takes on a physical body,
lets circumstances complete it.
That is why every being
spontaneously honors the Tao.

The Tao gives birth to all beings,
nourishes them, maintains them,
cares for them, comforts them, protects them,
takes them back to itself,
creating without possessing,
acting without expecting,
guiding without interfering.
That is why love of the Tao
is in the very nature of things.

(Chapter 51)

When employees say, "I love this place," what are they really saying? Simple: that they feel liberated to do their work as the best expression of themselves and their abilities. This chapter describes just such an environment, and the beauty of the text is the expression it gives to the exuberant joy of simply being allowed to be yourself.

Think of this reference to the Tao as the space the leader creates for each individual employee. And what characterizes this space? The first stanza emphasizes freedom as the key, describing it as an absolute freedom based on trust, a freedom not constrained by rules and restrictions.

The second stanza then describes a caring leadership that nurtures and supports but doesn't smother or possess with too much attention, that is also grounded in the freedom from intrusive, looking-over-the-shoulder supervision.

The proof of whether a leader has created a place of freedom and nurture is that the employees will honor that leader, spontaneously and unconsciously. You'll see it as good morale, productivity, and business results. And you'll hear it in such comments as "I love this place."

35

. . . Try to make people happy,
and you lay the groundwork for misery.
Try to make people moral,
and you lay the groundwork for vice.

Thus the Master is content
to serve as an example
and not to impose her will.
She is pointed, but doesn't pierce.
Straightforward, but supple.
Radiant, but easy on the eyes.

(from Chapter 58)

Be skeptical of the business leader who says, "In my company, we're just one big happy family." Chances are he's trying to control the employees, making the rules, then rewarding them when they obey and punishing them when they don't. But his focus is really on power over others, and his attempts to control people's behavior become repression. As one manager likes to put it, "Even in a happy family, you have to take out the trash and clean the toilets. If you have to do that at work, no one will be happy."

So put aside the family model as a way to create a productive workplace. You are leader and manager, not Big Daddy. Though there are managers who speak positively about the "parent model of management," it's very risky. To begin with, a family is bound by inextricable connections: you can't fire your children, so you can never have the same relationships with employees as with children. You have far more emotionally charged connections with your children than you should ever have with your employees. Otherwise, how could you do an honest appraisal without an employee feeling personally insulted, even as your children feel when you try to be objective with them?

The concept of family within the workplace also risks establishing unhealthy bonds of personal loyalty rather than professional loyalty. Managers who like to brag, "My people are loyal to me," are on the wrong track. Once you require employees' loyalty to you rather than to the larger purpose, you have reduced your potential for bringing out your employees' best results. Of course, their loyalty to the larger purpose may be informed by respect for you, but you should never evaluate them on the basis of their personal loyalties rather than their professional results. To do otherwise is to engage in favoritism.

You can't always love the people you work with, and you should be prepared to reward the good work of people you don't even like, or discipline people you do like. If you can't say, "I love you, you're fired," or, "You're a pain in the ass, here's your raise," you shouldn't be in management.

Be wary also of another popular metaphor for businesses: the team. It's true that the organization of work groups into teams has improved work for many people by involving them in an overall project rather than just a piece of something; it has also increased productivity. But this doesn't mean that companies or large departments should begin referring to themselves as teams. When that happens, senior executives begin to think of themselves as coaches and begin to think of their employees as superstars and benchwarmers. They think of winning and losing, of winners and losers. They use sports metaphors with all the images of blocking and tackling, of crushing the defenses, of kicking butt, and so on.

Wise leaders understand that the workplace is a community composed, as all communities are, of people whose abilities span a broad spectrum of competence. Managers like to claim, "All my people are outstanding," but they know it's nonsense even as they say it. Everyone has strengths and weaknesses, and the wise leader knows that her real job is, as Peter Drucker says, to make people's strengths effective and their weaknesses irrelevant. She doesn't do this with pep talks and slaps on the back, nor does she do it with sharp criticism and intimidation—all of which is ineffective for achieving long-term results. Instead, she creates clarity about what needs to be done and makes sure that everyone understands how individual jobs fit into the purpose of the organization.

Just as the wise leader realizes that external rewards don't make people happy, she understands that she can't *make* other people happy. She can only create a place in which they can be who they are, and if they have the capacity to find happiness in their work, they'll find it. But the wise leader is not naive or paralyzed by her ideals. Even when the workplace is the best it can be, she knows there still may be people who don't flourish, and people she will have to fire. Sometimes, firing those people, as difficult as it is, helps create a better workplace for the people who remain.

The wise leader is open with everyone, and she delights

in doing good, but she isn't self-conscious or self-righteous. Her mind is sharp, but she uses it to cut away difficulties, not to cut into people, and she remains supple in her response to ever-changing circumstances.

The wise leader realizes it is more effective, though more difficult, to live an exemplary life than to impose her ideals on others. Her radiant example doesn't make people think, "Wow! How brilliant she is!" but, "What a wonderful person she is! I think I can be that way too."

If you want to shrink something,
you must first allow it to expand.
If you want to get rid of something,
you must first allow it to flourish.

(from Chapter 36)

As with other chapters, the lessons of this one could apply to several different management situations. But let's consider a problem every manager faces from time to time: the unexpected outbreak of discontent. Left unchecked, of course, this can lead to serious morale problems.

Listen for the early signs. You've heard them; everyone has. They might be called "the whispers of discontent."

What are the symptoms? Little things at first, like derisive jokes on the bulletin board or e-mail. Then later, you may do an employee attitude survey and find yourself shocked by the negative comments. Or the boss walks in one day and asks, "Where do all these rumors get started?" If things get bad enough, open argument may break out, and the next thing you know, the human-resources people are breathing down your neck about seminars on conflict resolution.

How does all this begin? Workplaces are human communities, and people in every organization, no matter how well led, will become dissatisfied from time to time. But the whispers of discontent inevitably develop into morale and productivity problems when employees feel that they are not being heard.

Some managers don't take the whispers seriously enough. They still have the old attitude: "People are going to bitch about one thing or another, and there's nothing I can do about it." Other managers believe that employees want to see the world only from their own perspective and don't understand how things really work.

The issue is never how to get rid of all discontent, but how to deal with it in a way that shrinks it rather than pushes it into other, more disruptive forms, such as slowdowns and lower-quality work and efforts to organize against the company. If you want to keep the discontent to a minimum and avoid the larger problems, then you should stress honest communication, and you should provide a forum in which people can, without fear of recrimination or retribution, fully express their concerns and criticisms—even if the criticisms are about you. And you should listen without argument. The objective is to get to the source of the discontents, to examine the underlying causes. Are there issues of pay, working conditions, behavior problems by some people in the workplace? The forum itself is a move toward resolution of these issues, an opportunity for you as the leader to see everything affecting the employees, rather than just reacting to each problem as it arises. Even when there are issues you can't resolve immediately, it is often enough for people to know that you are there, you're listening, and you know what they're going through.

Some wise leaders meet informally with small groups, giving everyone a chance to speak in a minimally intimidating setting. Other leaders have departmental or group "town meetings," in which employees have access to open microphones or can submit anonymous comments and questions. In all settings, the emphasis is not on operations or planning, but on how the people are feeling about their jobs. And in all settings, there should be sufficient time for everyone who wants to speak.

The key is to create a safe place where people's discontents can be expressed in full voice. Sometimes, in these safe settings, the employees come to their own resolutions. If you don't try to force things to happen, but create opportunities in which things can happen naturally, and if you remain receptive, your employees will give of themselves wholeheartedly.

―37―

. . . The Master is available to all people
and doesn't reject anyone.
He is ready to use all situations
and doesn't waste anything. . . .

(from Chapter 27)

It's tempting to treat our top performers better than the marginal ones. That's okay when it comes to compensation and bonuses, but you should never withhold your good will from any employee. Treating all your employees with respect is the only way to bring out the best in everyone, even in those who are not so good. No workplace can be made up only of superstars, and managers who ignore the average, competent workers do so at the peril of their department's or company's long-term productivity. Managers too frequently put their most intense efforts into supporting and rewarding the superstars. Thus, these managers take their valuable training skills away from the people who need them most.

It's even more important to be aware of how you treat people when you have just acquired another company. The wise leader of an acquiring company understands and appreciates that the people who created an attractive company are the ones who made it worth acquiring in the first place. And he expresses his satisfaction that his people in the acquiring company have created an enterprise strong enough to take on another big challenge.

Many acquisitions fail to produce the results the acquiring company expected. Why? It's no secret. Too often, the managers in an acquiring company assume that they know the business better than the managers of the acquired company. In turn, the managers of the acquired company, already anxious about their fate, begin to think of their new bosses as the enemy. Proceeding without trust on either side, the acquirers, in their arrogance, begin to push the acquirees, who then become defensive. The focus on good work, productivity, and results gets lost in the political struggle, and everybody suffers.

Executives of acquiring companies put great quantities of time and energy into acquiring a company, but they rarely put the same effort into making the employees of the acquired company feel valued. The wise leader needs to make it clear to his own employees just what made the target company attractive and why the new employees are so important. He starts with building an appreciation for the people, their accomplishments, and their products. This should be a full-scale communications project in which people from the acquired company are brought in to make presentations and to get acquainted. The wise leader does the same thing for employees and officers of the acquired company. In both settings, there should be great emphasis on positive accomplishments and on what the two groups can learn from each other.

This kind of leadership is the least disruptive to people and operations, it builds a reputation that makes other companies respond enthusiastically to the possibility of being acquired, and it produces superior business results.

38

The Tao never does anything,
yet through it all things are done.

If powerful men and women
could center themselves in it,
the whole world would be transformed
by itself, in its natural rhythms.
People would be content
with their simple, everyday lives,
in harmony, and free of desire.

When there is no desire,
all things are at peace.

(Chapter 37)

One of the Tao Te Ching's great contributions is to challenge our ways of looking not only at the world but also at the words we use in describing what we see. For instance, the word *contentment* is often defined negatively as complacency. Of course, we don't want a workplace filled with people who are complacent, who have no passion for excellence, who are just satisfied with the status quo. On the other hand, we don't want a workplace filled with upward-striving, self-serving, back-stabbing workers concerned only with their own ambitions.

But in this chapter, "content" is equivalent to "in harmony" and means "happy, fulfilled, deeply accepting of things as they are."

But you might ask, "What motivates people like this to go the extra mile when the company is really under pressure, when we need some special effort?" The answer lies in the phrase "who love their work." The people motivate themselves. They gain enormous energy from the group dynamic, from the workplace community itself. This is not a matter of external motivation; you should get beyond the old saw that external values are the only things that make people productive. Let go of the assumption that in order to get people to do good work you have to drive them to it with money and promotions.

This is not to say that external rewards don't have value; they do, but only in the short term. For people to be happy in the long term, work must be its own reward. Otherwise, people spend their lives chasing the phantoms of money and power, and lose their focus on the internal values that give them their true rewards.

You help people find these true rewards by affirming them and their work and by helping them connect what they do with the greater purposes of the organization. One leader works with people to develop individual statements of purpose that directly tie to the company's statement of purpose. "If people are to find meaning in their work," he says, "they must feel that it makes a difference by being connected to what we're trying to accomplish together."

Attention to purpose and connection provides the foundation for long-term commitment, and provides a context in which external rewards are more effective. But if you depend only on external rewards for positive motivation, along with critique and discipline as negative motivation, you'll spend your life in carrot-and-stick management.

In business we accept too easily the conventional wisdom we have created. "Ambition" is good, "contentment" is bad; "desire" is good, "satisfaction" is bad. The wise leader realizes that the first obligation of leadership is to help people find meaning in their work, no matter what the job. Whether the employees are sorting the mail, directing the sales force, sweeping up the floor, or chairing the board of directors meetings, they should be able to find meaning in their work.

Then the people will develop a *passion* for the work and for the greater purpose of the organization. This is different from *desire*, which is in service of the ego.

Think about it. What could be more productive than a company staffed with happy people who love their simple, everyday lives, who don't feel obsessed or driven, who are mutually supportive and delighted with their leadership, who love their work but can leave it behind and give themselves fully to the other passions of their lives: family, friends, and community?

39

Whoever is planted in the Tao
will not be rooted up.
Whoever embraces the Tao
will not slip away.
Her name will be held in honor
from generation to generation. . . .

(from Chapter 54)

T hink about the business leaders you have most admired, the ones you most want to emulate. Who are they? The effective cost-cutters? The competent administrators? The talented technicians? Perhaps, but not likely. While the great leaders may have been effective, competent, and talented, their most admirable traits—openness, honesty, trust, and the courage to do the right thing—had more to do with who they were as people than with what they did as professionals.

When people are asked to describe the leaders they have admired and learned from, you never hear, "He was always able to achieve a superior return on stockholder equity." Instead, you hear them talk about these leaders' human qualities: stories of their personal contacts, their special attention in times of need, their community volunteer work. You hear, "He was a wonderful man." Or "She always seemed to be able to sense when I had a personal problem."

A few years ago, when downsizing was becoming a fad, the CEO of a major corporation called all his senior department heads together. "I've heard that some of you think we should cut costs by jumping on the downsizing bandwagon. I agree we need to address our cost structure, but I want you to come up with the most creative ideas you can for doing it. As for those of you who feel that laying off our employees is the best way to do it, I suggest that you may not be comfortable working in the _____ Corporation. Our employees have built this company, and I would consider it immoral to lay off any of them before we've tried everything else first."

This story has become part of that corporation's story. The company has done well, the CEO is still there, and you may rest assured that his name will be held in honor there for generations.

There was another executive, a senior vice president of one of the world's largest corporations, who decided he'd had enough of the command/control model. "It just wasn't me," he explained. "I myself always did better, performed better, when I was seeing to my own personal growth and having a lot of say-so in how I did my work."

So this VP took a big risk. He decided to make personal growth one of the performance standards for all his people. "I knew if I only 'encouraged' them," he said with a laugh, "they might not trust that they should really do it. So I made it part of their job." He called his senior managers together for a conference at which he staged a personal-growth fair. There were booths featuring all kinds of community volunteer opportunities, as well as orientation courses and demonstrations of the soft martial arts and meditation, plus materials from mainstream churches. His idea was to expose his people to the possibilities, to let them choose something new or simply reaffirm whatever they were already doing. But he required that they write it into their performance standards. "If they said, 'I'm going to spend more time with my kids,'" he explained, "that would have been okay. But I wanted the commitment, because I know that people who are growing personally are also maintaining the kind of balance that makes them good, productive long-term employees."

These executives were truly living what this chapter calls for: the admirable traits of consistency, authenticity, and balance in both life and work.

What you do is transient, but who you essentially are will never slip away.

40

We join spokes together in a wheel,
but it is the center hole
that makes the wagon move.

We shape clay into a pot,
but it is the emptiness inside
that holds whatever we want.

We hammer wood for a house,
but it is the inner space
that makes it livable.

We work with being,
but non-being is what we use.

(Chapter 11)

The powerful, everyday images of this text make a point that may seem mystical at first but is actually quite obvious upon reflection, something that we all intuitively know.

We use materials and techniques to make a wheel or a pot or a house—yet what makes them useful is not their form but the space that their form defines and creates. A room is what is inside its four walls; the walls make the room possible but they aren't the room. Even what is inside the room—its furniture, lighting, floor coverings, and so on—only accommodates how people live within the room; they are not the living itself.

So what does that have to do with management? Just this: in business we attempt to see the things we can't see by creating structures we can see. Then we become preoccupied with the structure rather than what happens within that structure. There are corporate strategic planning departments, for instance, who are far more concerned with whether a plan conforms to the established format than with the quality of the thinking reflected in the plan. We've asked this question many times already: Is the organizational chart the actual organization? Managers want to believe that the chart they create shows the interrelationships of the people, how communication and power flow among them. But this is an illusion. Whether the structure is shown as a circle, cross-functional teams, self-managed teams, or a traditional pyramid, the idea is to show people in relationships according to that diagram. But the organization isn't that diagram; the true organization can't be seen, because it is the energy and commitment generated by people working in relationships that results in products and services for the customers. And in fact, what the customer buys is only the tangible manifestation of this same energy and commitment of the people.

There is a physical-resource aspect to this as well. Managers provide employees with all the equipment, the offices, the desks, the computers, and so on, to do the job. As important as these resources are, they don't accomplish anything.

Most companies operate in spite of structure rather than because of it. Sometimes employees will even become more of an effective tight-knit community in their reaction *against* the bureaucracy. In the old army, for instance, it was the top sergeants who knew how to find the loopholes in the regulations so the work could get done. In today's corporations it is the senior secretaries and clerical workers who oil the mechanisms of the daily workplace and keep things moving.

Of course, it is vital that a leader be adept at determining the appropriate structure and resources for every situation. But it is even more important that the leader not become enslaved by these things and not hold her employees hostage to form. She must instead understand the power of what she doesn't do, and value the things she can't see.

Part V
Vision

—41—

*. . . If powerful men and women
could remain centered in the Tao,
all things would be in harmony.
The world would become a paradise.
All people would be at peace,
and the law would be written in their
  hearts. . . .*

(from Chapter 32)

I f we were to live our lives and manage our businesses according to the principles in the Tao Te Ching, how would business be? How would *you* answer?

This chapter may appear to promise a Utopia; surely the world could never be that way. Or could it? If not the world, couldn't our own personal lives and businesses be that way?

How Utopian is it to imagine that wise leaders could create workplaces of support and not of fear, workplaces that are truly communities, in which people's needs are honored and their professional achievements rewarded? It should be obvious by now that short-term, quarter-to-quarter thinking has moved from the senior executives to managers at all levels, causing them to respond in many ways to the calls for cost cutting: they sacrifice future product development for short-term financial gain; they cut back on equipment and resources; they squeeze down the size of salary increases; and they refuse to replace people who resign. Many managers are realizing that short-term thinking will inevitably undercut their future, but with no other formula for success, businesses are scrambling to find a way out of the problem they've created for themselves. Business leaders look to management fads and gimmicks for quick answers without paying attention to the people they're imposing them on: the employees whose creative power makes the company run. In this way, they're like the oil prospector who, while unknowingly sitting on the richest land in the world, sends agents out to foreign countries to look for what he's already got. Your greatest resource—the people who work for you—is right under your nose.

As long as companies think of employees as costs rather than assets, they will always be tempted to reduce the costs rather than invest further in the assets by providing safety nets for health care, retirement, and all the things that help people get through their lives with dignity. The return on those investments will be workers who are dedicated and highly productive because they feel valued.

How Utopian is it to imagine that there could be open and honest relationships throughout business, between managers and employees and with stockholders, vendors, customers, and the community at large?

It is the desire for power that causes manipulation of information. Yet it's clear that dishonesty and secrecy don't pay. Witness how many downsizings were announced to financial analysts and the press but not directly to employees, who then waited with great anxiety to see which of them would get the ax. The result was anger and bitterness, bad press, threatened political action. And to the surprise of many of those companies, downsizing didn't bring gains in market share, productivity, or market value. In an ironic comment in the mid-nineties, after several years of downsizings, one of the people responsible for the theories behind the layoff fad said, "We didn't seem to give sufficient consideration to the human side of the equation."

If staff reductions are necessary, as they sometimes are for the survival of the enterprise, there is even a way to make layoffs in accordance with the Tao Te Ching. It starts with honesty, with expressions of regret, and with admissions of management mistakes; then it continues with direct person-to-person communication with the people to be laid off; and it concludes with outplacement services, fair and equitable severance packages, and continuation of health benefits for a reasonable period. This approach would benefit the people who are being downsized, of course, but it also would be reassuring to the people who remain and upon whom the company will depend for even more commitment and productivity.

The wise leader realizes that when he is centered in the Tao, his company becomes centered in the Tao. And when one company is centered in the Tao, it becomes that much more possible for the rest of the world.

42

The Tao doesn't take sides;
it gives birth to both good and evil.
The Master doesn't take sides;
she welcomes both saints and sinners.

The Tao is like a bellows:
it is empty yet infinitely capable.
The more you use it, the more it produces;
the more you talk of it, the less you understand.

Hold on to the center.

(Chapter 5)

We've pointed many times to the difficulties created by categories and preconceptions. What happens when we turn them against each other in our business lives? Managers often divide their world into opposites—workers versus managers, union workers versus non-union workers, my department versus the accounting department or the human-resources department, my project versus the other project. If you take sides and let yourself get caught up in opposites, you can't be effective. This chapter says that the appropriate approach to wise leadership is to always be in a state of receptivity, in which no person is judged good or bad, saint or sinner, and no idea is judged right or wrong in advance.

Think about it. The world of nature is in itself an undivided system, not a collection of opposites always acting one against another. Night is not the enemy of day, for example, nor is energy the opposite of matter: they are different aspects of the same thing. But people resist thinking of the world like that. We are more comfortable with the belief that nature is about the survival of the fittest. Thus we think of business as that kind of competitive do-or-die world. But try thinking of your business as a whole, without emphasizing, say, sales so that you forget the people who create what they sell, without focusing only on star performers so that you forget the majority of non-stars who are mostly responsible for making your department or company function day to day. Business is a wonderful interplay of people—stockholders, employees, customers, vendors—their ideas and their work.

After all, despite what is said about the independence of the free market, business still exists in a complex economic, political, and social ecosystem. Often business people seem to forget that their employees and the employees of other companies (including their competitors) are also customers and stockholders.

True vision isn't one-dimensional; it means considering all viewpoints and recognizing opponents as challenges rather than as enemies. The benefits of this kind of thinking should be clear by now—act as if someone is an enemy, and you'll create an enemy; respect others as worthy opponents, and you'll create a healthy industry. The wise leader remains flexible, open-minded to all ideas and opinions, and open-hearted to all people.

Like a bellows, the wise leader remains primarily in a state of emptiness, ready at any moment to be filled with creative energy, capable of being productive over and over again. If you can think this way, you can empty yourself of preconceptions about business tactics or people's abilities and begin to accept ideas from anyone, at any level. You can empty yourself of ego protection and begin to trust everyone. You can empty yourself of judgment and be flexible about work habits and behavior. And you can empty yourself of notions about power and accept your people as they are.

— 43 —

What is rooted is easy to nourish.
What is recent is easy to correct. . . .

Prevent trouble before it arises.
Put things in order before they exist.
The giant pine tree
grows from a tiny sprout.
The journey of a thousand miles
starts from beneath your feet. . . .

(from Chapter 64)

Everything needs a strong beginning. Whether you're sending a youngster off to his first day of school, hiring a new employee, or launching a major new product, you should be aware that everything is most vulnerable at its beginning. That's obvious. What's not so obvious are the ways you can create successful beginnings. In this chapter, the Tao Te Ching pays special attention to this subject. Indeed, one of the most quoted sentences from the book is "The journey of a thousand miles starts from beneath your feet."

The questions of when to act and what form the action should take are a constant challenge to every leader. This is very tricky, particularly in business, because it's often so difficult to define when something actually begins. For instance, what's the beginning of a new product launch? At the research stage or the design stage? Testing? Management approval and planning? Manufacturing? Packaging? Or is it when you go public with advertising and promotion, when you show it to customers for the first time? In fact, every one of these stages, plus others, has its own separate beginning, and all of them add up to an overall "beginning."

Every new thing must have a conceptual process and a plan, or it will fail for lack of a pattern. If in the development of something you perceive that it is in good shape and ready to grow, you need to nourish it so that it can put down its roots. This is true of a marketing plan or a manufacturing process. Conversely, if you perceive something negative about it, you can correct that quality much more easily if you do it before it puts down roots.

Timing is always the essential issue. Just when has something put down roots? It is important to determine the maturation time of anything you undertake, because once it's on course, you have to let it grow at its own pace. As with a plant, sometimes the best help you can give it is watchful attention. Too much water or sunlight might kill it. The worst thing you can do is force it to a premature conclusion.

It's also true that, despite everything you do to prevent trouble before it arises, a project can still head for disaster. When this happens, you may just have to blow the whistle on it, cut and run, salvage what you can. But salvaging means conserving as many resources as possible, rather than trying to force something forward just for the sake of your ego.

The wise leader does everything possible to foster the optimal conditions for strong beginnings. He concentrates on providing the open space in which creative possibilities can arise, the space in which everyone can be whoever they are. Thus he supports and nurtures people in a way that lets them develop at the best possible pace: their own.

. . . The Master lets all things come and go
effortlessly, without desire.
She never expects results;
thus she is never disappointed.
She is never disappointed;
thus her spirit never grows old.

(from Chapter 55)

In 1996, the CEO of a multibillion-dollar American company stated in a speech to stock-market analysts that he expected the company's earnings to rise at least ten percent a quarter during the coming year. The analysts, responding as they do to such predictions, recommended the stock, which then increased in price. But the earnings didn't rise as spectacularly as predicted, and the stock price went down.

As a result, the CEO sent a memo to the company's employees saying that they had embarrassed him and that he was disappointed in them. Never mind that if anyone was an embarrassment, it was he himself. The point here is that, by investing his ego in an unrealistic outcome, the CEO set himself up for failure, then projected that failure onto others, creating an entirely unnecessary melodrama that in turn disrupted the company and made a happy outcome even less probable.

Lower-level managers also create these blame-the-people and shoot-the-messenger problems, often without being aware that they're doing it. Sales managers in particular are often guilty of inflating sales goals for the sake of looking good during the budgeting and planning process, then when the goals are not met, the managers never say they overreached; they say the people underperformed.

The wise leader doesn't make empty promises based on nothing but her desire to force an outcome. She knows that results depend on the people, and she accepts whatever outcome there is. She doesn't invest her ego in expectations, and she doesn't project failure onto others. Thus she is never disappointed, and her spirit remains fresh, vigorous, and youthful.

— 45 —

Nothing in the world
is as soft and yielding as water.
Yet for dissolving the hard and inflexible,
nothing can surpass it.

The soft overcomes the hard;
the gentle overcomes the rigid. . . .

(from Chapter 78)

Don't let first impressions fool you. Things often aren't what they seem. Traditional management attitudes have always favored the hiring of men instead of women because women have been judged too soft for the power jobs. But just as water, soft and yielding, can carve mountains and deep valleys and can move millions of tons of topsoil across thousands of miles, people who are supple have no need to express power forcefully and can bring about enormous change in creating great organizations.

It depends on how we perceive manifestations of power. In most traditional settings, managers want to see power in the workplace as a directive attitude that establishes the manager's dominance over the employees. But if you see power as deriving from the results people are able to achieve, then that power can come about because the leader has been supple and has made people feel like participating rather than being driven. This is not necessarily a matter of gender, but it seems true that women are more likely than men to use the yielding power of participation rather than the top-down power of intimidation.

A very command/control male president of a large operating group was fired because he made one autocratic decision too many. It turned out to be a huge and costly mistake. His key people knew better, of course, and were opposed to the decision, but their choice was either to go along or get out.

The company replaced him with a very accomplished woman. One of her first moves was to create a forum for discussion of the group's problems and opportunities. She convened the first management conference the group had ever had, putting traditionally competitive department heads together in problem-solving teams. There was some grumbling about her "New Age, touchy-feely" approach, but she just kept inviting participation until even the most jaded managers began to get involved. In being supple and yielding, however, she was anything but wishy-washy. She fired some managers who were hanging on to their own power trips, and she reorganized several support departments. The group has improved its market share and is back on the road to full recovery. This is water moving topsoil.

. . . The Master is detached from all things;
that is why she is one with them.
Because she has let go of herself,
she is perfectly fulfilled.

(from Chapter 7)

C reativity is easily the most talked-about and least understood aspect of business life. We know that creativity isn't limited to jobs traditionally defined as "creative" but can be at the heart of every kind of work, whether it involves writing computer code, producing videos, doing complex sales presentations, or sorting the mail. Creativity can make ordinary work extraordinary and can turn mere competence into productive commitment.

Wouldn't it be wonderful if managers were taught how to encourage creativity? But they're not. In fact, the very characteristics that define creativity are the characteristics that make managers uncomfortable. In any field, the people who follow the conventional wisdom, who obey all the rules, who conform to all the policies and procedures, who make managers most comfortable are *not* the creative geniuses.

A truly wise leader, abandoning the traditional comfort

zone of management, understands that the source of all creative energy is beyond space and time. It can't be named or defined, yet it is the most real thing in the world, infinite and available to everyone. Part of the leader's job is to remain detached—in other words, to get out of the employees' way, so that they have ample opportunity to make the connection with their own creativity.

Being "detached from all things" seems at first to be a negative concept. But "detached" doesn't mean separate or uninvolved. It means not attached to any particular outcome, not identified with any particular part of the whole, not swept up in the temporary dramas of succeeding or failing.

One of the biggest blunders a leader can make is to become personally identified with a process or a specific desired outcome. Inevitably this will prejudice any action and inhibit creativity, because the manager will allocate resources—time, money, attention—to the potential outcome that most fits her preconceptions. Then what happens? The employees aren't dumb; they will quickly identify the boss's pet project and devote their energies to it so that they will be smiled upon. This might inflate the boss's ego, but it might also mean that a superior project was passed over in favor of the one the boss liked.

And who knows how many superior products have ended up in the trash bin of business because they couldn't get the attention of the top managers? Think also of how many employees took their rejected ideas and formed their own competitive companies. This has happened in industries as diverse as publishing, advertising, industrial machinery, all kinds of service businesses, and most dramatically in computer hardware and software development.

So, as difficult at it is, one of the most important things the leader can do to foster creativity is to cultivate within herself an attitude of detachment, remaining open to all possible outcomes and not becoming invested in any one of them.

But wait a minute. Is the text saying that the manager shouldn't express her own creativity and throw herself into what she loves and has a passion for, such as a particular project in which she is willing to invest herself and take the accompanying risks?

A good question, and at some point the manager/leader must do just that. But her first priority should be to create an atmosphere and provide the resources for people to pursue *their* passions. The leader's passion is for this vision of the whole, and her greatest fulfillment comes from the accomplishments of the people.

The Master gives himself up
to whatever the moment brings.
He knows that he is going to die,
and he has nothing left to hold on to:
no illusions in his mind,
no resistances in his body.
He doesn't think about his actions;
they flow from the core of his being.
He holds nothing back from life;
therefore he is ready for death,
as a man is ready for sleep
after a good day's work.

(Chapter 50)

There are business leaders who would never deny that everything is going to change but who still want to be sure that, after all the changes, their leadership will always be remembered. They try to control the change, to put limits on it, to assure that the management style or the organizational system which they have developed remains intact, so that they will be immortalized in the company.

Of course, it can be disorienting to realize that the vast majority of us are going to be forgotten no matter how terrific we may have been during our tenure with our companies. If we could project ourselves twenty years into the future, we probably wouldn't even recognize our companies or the businesses in which we've spent our careers. But there is a way to embrace this reality.

This chapter, at its most basic level, is a wonderful lesson on how to live in full acceptance of the transience of life. There are insights as well about the acceptance of the transient nature of the business life.

A wise leader, whether the CEO or a middle manager, understanding that continuity and transience are two sides of the same coin, doesn't deny that change is inevitable. He realizes that the worst thing he can do for his company or his department is to become so invested in its present form that he limits the natural flow of the business. Hanging on to provisional forms and trying to control how things will develop is a matter of ego, a kind of grasping at immortality: "If I can assure that this form, this structure, this business style endures, then my influence on this enterprise will always be recognized."

The wise leader isn't concerned about whether his influence will be recognized, only whether it will be a healthy influence as long as it is relevant. He's not scared that change will leave him behind. He doesn't pay attention to his so-called place in history. He isn't worried that when the company's story is written his name might not appear prominently. It's petty considerations like these that cause people to hang on tight to whatever they think made them successful in the first place. Then they fail to grow, and they become more irrelevant as the business grows.

The wise leader knows that, sooner or later, the business will go on without him. So what? Uninhibited by the caution that ego produces, he takes each day as it comes, holding back nothing from his engagement with life and work. He embraces new ideas, he mentors younger people, he helps his organization grow even when that means giving up some of the plans he worked so hard to develop.

And he never has the slightest problem sleeping.

─48─

. . . The Master has no possessions.
The more he does for others,
the happier he is.
The more he gives to others,
the wealthier he is.

The Tao nourishes by not forcing.
By not dominating, the Master leads.

(from Chapter 81)

So how do you become a wise leader?

Are there numerous and complex rules to master? No. There aren't any rules. There is only a way of being.

If you use this little book as a guide, all you need to do is look inside yourself and determine what you should let go of, then let go of it every day.

The desire to know? Let go of it. Practice beginner's mind. Learn how to not-know.

The need to be in control? Let go of it. Control is an illusion. The more you seek it, the more it will evade you.

The ambition for power, money, and prestige? Let go of it. What you already have is enough. Accept rewards if they come your way, but accept them only as symbols of your good work.

Remember that a wise leader isn't a victim of his ego; thus, he makes no one else a victim. Instead of forcing his ideas and expectations on others, he creates a space in which others can do their own good work.

Above all, the wise leader is a resource for others. He serves, supports, and nurtures the people around him.

Mindful that true words seem paradoxical when the mind is cluttered with untruth, the wise leader embraces paradox.

By not forcing, he leads.

By not dominating, he leads.

By not leading, he leads.

Resources

Readers who are interested in encountering the entire text of the Tao Te Ching in a version by one coauthor of this book are referred to *Tao Te Ching: A New English Version*, with Foreword and Notes, by Stephen Mitchell, HarperCollins, 1988.

James Autry, the author of three previous books about leadership, works with business and nonprofit organizations all over the country as a speaker and workshop leader on the subjects of honesty, trust, courage, and balance. He has two training videos available, including the award-winning *Love and Profit*.

For more information, call (515) 279-1245. You may also write to him at PO Box 12069, Des Moines, IA 50312; or send e-mail to JAutrydsm@AOL.com. Or check his Web page at http://members.AOL.com/Jamesautry.

The two training programs for business leaders described below take into action the principles discussed in *Real Power*. The mindfulness meditation taught in both programs was prominently featured in the Bill Moyers PBS special *Healing and the Mind.*

Wisdom at Work

The Project on Contemplative Mind in Society, a joint venture of the Nathan Cummings Foundation and the Fetzer Institute, has been developing a program of mindfulness practice in business. It is an exploration for business executives and employees of the personal and the professional and the relationship between the two. The program includes mindfulness meditation practice in retreats created especially for the business community and in the workplace, ways to sustain mindfulness in daily life, and the development of support materials.

For more information on this program, write to:

Wisdom at Work
Contemplative Mind in Society
38 Village Hill Road
Williamsburg, MA 01096
Telephone: (413) 268-7236
E-mail: seva@crocker.com

The Power of Mindfulness: A Transformative Retreat for CEOs and Emerging Corporate Leaders

The Stress Reduction Clinic and the Center for Mindfulness in Medicine, Health Care, and Society at the University of Massachusetts Medical Center offer five-day intensive retreats for CEOs and top-level corporate executives. These retreats are held in beautiful settings and consist of rigorous training in mindfulness meditation and its practical applications for enhanced personal creativity, for understanding personal and organizational stress and developing effective ways of preventing and responding to it, and ultimately, for making work work better at all levels of an organization.

The Center for Mindfulness also offers a range of on-site mindfulness-based stress-reduction programs for corporate clients.

For more information, write or call:

The Center for Mindfulness
Corporate Programs
UMass Medical Center
419 Belmont Street
Worcester, MA 01604
Telephone: (508) 856-4057
Fax: (508) 856-1977

"Mindfulness," according to Dr. Jon Kabat-Zinn, Executive Director of the Center for Mindfulness and founding director of the Stress Reduction Clinic, "is best described as moment-to-moment, non-judgmental awareness. It is cultivated by intentionally attending to the present moment in particular by paying attention to those aspects of our bodies, our minds, and our lives that we so often most take for granted, from our own breathing and body sensations to our perceptions, thoughts, opinions, and emotions, and those of others. The practice of mindfulness can be profoundly transformative and healing. It can give rise to greater insight and clarity, as well as greater empathy for oneself and for others. It can help us be more in touch with our own deepest and most trustworthy characteristics, reminding us of what is most important in business, in our own lives, and in the lives of those we most love and care for. Mindfulness can make it easier for us to experience the web of interconnectedness in which we live and work, and use our understanding of that interconnectedness to make more effective and wiser choices as we continue to learn and grow across the lifespan."

Acknowledgments

We would like to express our gratitude to our editor, Amy Hertz, whose fierce dedication and X-ray eyes helped shape this book; to Michael Katz and Rafe Sagalyn, our excellent agents; to our beloved wives, Vicki Chang and Sally Pederson; and to Lao-tzu, who made it all possible.

James A. Autry, a former Fortune 500 executive, is an award-winning business author and one of the most popular and influential consultants in the business community.

Stephen Mitchell is a bestselling author and translator. His translation of Tao Te Ching and his interpretation of its principles are used in this book.